Mindfulness in Behavioral Health

Series Editor
Nirbhay N. Singh
Medical College of Georgia,
Georgia Regents University,
Augusta, Georgia,
USA

More information about this series at http://www.springer.com/series/8678

Yoon-Suk Hwang • Patrick Kearney

A Mindfulness Intervention for Children with Autism Spectrum Disorder

New Directions in Research and Practice

Springer

Yoon-Suk Hwang
Australian Catholic University
Banyo
Queensland
Australia

Patrick Kearney
Kalyana Mitta Sanga
Highgate Hill
Queensland
Australia

ISSN 2195-9579 ISSN 2195-9587 (electronic)
Mindfulness in Behavioral Health
ISBN 978-3-319-18961-1 ISBN 978-3-319-18962-8 (eBook)
DOI 10.1007/978-3-319-18962-8

Library of Congress Control Number: 2015940426

Springer Cham Heidelberg New York Dordrecht London

Printed on acid-free paper

Springer International Publishing AG Switzerland is part of Springer Science+Business Media (www.springer.com)

We would like to express our gratitude to the mothers and their children who participated in this project, Cultivating Mind and Enhancing Life.

Contents

About the Authors

Yoon-Suk Hwang, Ph.D., is a research fellow at the Learning Sciences Institute Australia (LSIA), Australian Catholic University. Prior to this role she was a lecturer in inclusive and special education at Griffith University. As an experienced mindfulness practitioner with a research expertise in listening to the voices of people living with developmental disabilities, she has applied mindfulness to address the behavioural problems of learners with autism spectrum disorders (ASD) and to enhance the quality of their family life. Dr. Hwang began her teacher training in special education in 1996 and worked as a special education teacher of a support class in an inclusive primary school. She received a Ph.D. in 2009 from the University of Sydney based on a thesis, Mind and Autism Spectrum Disorders: A Theory-of-Mind Continuum Model and Typology Developed from Theory-of-Mind as Subjectively Experienced and Objectively Understood. She has recently extended this project to Singaporean and Australian students with ASD and their parents and teachers.

Patrick Kearney is an independent dharma teacher in the lineage of Mahasi Sayadaw of Myanmar, a key figure in the modern revival of insight meditation and mindfulness training. Mr. Kearney began meditation practice in 1976, and since 1984 has trained extensively in the Mahasi approach to insight meditation. This included several years as an ordained Buddhist monk. He has also trained in the Diamond Sangha lineage of Zen Buddhism and has studied early Buddhism at postgraduate levels. He continues to study Pali, the language of the earliest surviving Indian recension of the Buddha's teachings. Mr. Kearney has a particular interest in the original teachings of the Buddha, before "Buddhism" began, and seeks to bring his understanding of the early texts to the practice of dharma and meditation in the contemporary world.

About the Authors

List of Abbreviations

AN	Aṅguttara Nikāya
DN	Dīgha Nikāya
MN	Majjhima Nikāya
SN	Saṃyutta Nikāya
Ud	Udāna
Khp	Khuddakapātha

Some of the data provided here was initially published in Y-S Hwang, Kearney, P., Klieve, H., Lang, W. & Roberts, J. (2015). Cultivating Mind: Mindfulness interventions for children with autism spectrum disorder and problem behaviours, and their mothers. DOI 10.1007/s10826-015-0114-x. *Journal of Child and Family Studies*.

Chapter 1
Introduction

The demands of raising a child with autism spectrum disorder (ASD) entail a steep learning curve for parents as they devote much of their time, attention and energy to learning about their child's characteristics and how to secure the best support and services (Stoner et al., 2005). While parenting a child with ASD can be "rewarding" and a "privilege", bringing out the best in parents, the day-to-day challenges they experience can also be "exhausting" and "stressful" (Glazzard & Overall, 2012, p. 40). Parents need to develop a wide variety of skills to manage the issues that arise from their child's ASD, especially given the extreme individuality of the disorder (Bearss et al., 2013; Oono Honey, & McConachie, 2013). These difficulties tend to worsen when their child has challenging behaviours, and appropriate social support services are not in place (McGill Papachristoforou, & Cooper, 2006).

Recent intervention studies have reported the successful application of mindfulness meditation practice for individuals with developmental disability (DD), including ASD, as evidenced by reductions in their behavioural (e.g. Singh et al., 2013), psychological (e.g. Spek et al., 2013) and physical (e.g. Singh et al., 2014a) problems. Mindfulness interventions for individuals with DD can be traced back to 2003, when Singh and his colleagues conducted a 12-month mindfulness intervention that resulted in reductions in thc aggressive behaviours of an adult with intellectual disability (ID) and mental illness who was in danger of losing his community living arrangement because of his uncontrolled aggressive behaviour.

The initial work of Singh Wahler, Adkins and Myers (2003) was extended by follow-up studies that demonstrated the positive effects of mindfulness training for both people with DD (e.g. Singh et al., 2011, 2014a), and their family and professional care providers (e.g. Bazzano et al., 2015; Bethay et al., 2013). In addition, indirect effects of mindfulness training for family or professional care providers were reported for their care recipients with DD (e.g. Neece, 2014; Singh et al., 2009). Recent mindfulness intervention studies (e.g. Idusohan-Moizer Sawicka, Dendle, & Albany, 2015; Sakdalan Shaw, & Collier, 2010) have extended their objectives and diversified their content by applying existing mindfulness-based intervention programmes (MBIs), such as mindfulness-based cognitive therapy (MBCT) and

Y.-S. Hwang, P. Kearney, *A Mindfulness Intervention for Children with Autism Spectrum Disorder*, Mindfulness in Behavioral Health,
DOI 10.1007/978-3-319-18962-8_1

dialectical behaviour therapy (DBT), to enhance the behavioural and psychological well-being of individuals with DD.

Mindfulness interventions have become both more numerous and more diverse in their application to the physical, behavioural and/or psychological health of people affected by a range of conditions, including disabilities. The growing prominence of this field of study has prompted a reappraisal of the fundamentals of mindfulness practice as a component of the social and health sciences, to ensure that the theoretical and practical foundations have been properly laid to support any future expansion of the field of mindfulness studies (e.g. Gethin, 2011; Williams & Kabat-Zinn, 2011).

When mindfulness was first applied to people suffering chronic health problems (Kabat-Zinn, 1990), the priority was to create an effective practice package that could ameliorate the suffering of practitioners, and the main theoretical concern was to present mindfulness as a secular practice that could fit within a scientific context. As the field has developed, however, the theoretical understanding that frames the concepts of mindfulness and its practice has not been as strongly developed (Grossman, 2011). In a recent study, for example, Singh and his colleagues (Singh et al., 2014b) have called attention to the need for a second generation of mindfulness interventions, based in part on a deeper understanding of the traditional roots of mindfulness practice.

The current intervention could be located within this emerging second generation of mindfulness studies. We begin in Chap. 2 with a genealogy of mindfulness that traces the development of the concept from its origins in the early teachings of the Buddha to its application to contemporary health and social sciences. We continue in Chap. 3 with a systematic literature review of mindfulness intervention studies conducted for individuals living with DD, examination of the trends of current mindfulness intervention and research practices and identification of areas of strengths and improvements.

Based on the understanding of mindfulness outlined in Chap. 2, and addressing the issues that arose from Chap. 3, then in Chap. 4 we will report on the development and delivery of the first stage of the current mindfulness programme. This intervention is structured around six mother–child dyads, where the children are characterized by ASD and challenging behaviours. The first stage of the study aimed to train the six mothers to a level of fluency in mindfulness practice so that they could both apply mindfulness to their own lives and become mindfulness teachers for their own child.

In Chap. 5, we will report on the second stage of this study, in which these mothers transition to become mindfulness teachers to their own children, at first with the support of the researchers and then independently. Here, we apply contemporary educational theories (e.g. differentiations and self-determination) and practices (e.g. parent-implemented intervention and video modelling) to create an initial mindfulness training programme appropriate for the specific needs and characteristics of these six children. Chapters 4 and 5 will include a report on the results of the intervention as it affected mothers and children both directly, through their own mindfulness practice, and indirectly, through their reciprocal relationships with their family members who practised mindfulness.

Results are discussed in Chap. 6 and compared to those of previous mindfulness intervention studies. We conclude our work by exploring the implications of the results and areas that future mindfulness studies need to address to advance our ways of supporting the lives of people living with DD.

References

Bazzano, A., Wolfe, C., Zylowska, L., Wang, S., Shchuster, E., Barrett, C., & Lehrer, D. (2015). Mindfulness based stress reduction (MBSR) for parents and caregivers of individuals with developmental disabilities: A community-based approach. *Journal of Child and Family Studies, 24,* 298–308. doi:10.1007/s10826-013-9836-9.

Bearss, K., Lecavalier, L., Minshawl, N., Johnson, C., Smith, T., Handen, B., & Scahill, L. (2013). Toward an exportable parent training program for disruptive behaviours in autism spectrum disorder. *Neuropsychiatry, 3*(2), 169–180.

Bethay, J. S., Wilson, K. G., Schnetzer, L. W., Nassar, S. I., & Bordieri, M. J. (2013). A controlled pilot evaluation of acceptance and commitment training for intellectual disability staff. *Mindfulness, 4,* 113–121.

Gethin, R. M. L. (2011). On some definitions of mindfulness. *Contemporary Buddhism, 12*(1), 263–279.

Glazzard, J., & Overall, K. (2012). Living with autistic spectrum disorder: Parental experiences of raising a child with autistic spectrum disorder (ASD). *British Journal of Learning Support, 27*(1), 37–45.

Grossman, P. (2011). Defining mindfulness by how poorly I think I pay attention during everyday awareness and other intractable problems for psychology's (re)invention of mindfulness: Comment on Brown et al. (2011). *Psychological Assessment, 23*(4), 1034–1040.

Idusohan-Moizer, H., Sawicka, A., Dendle, J., & Albany, M. (2015). Mindfulness-based cognitive therapy for adults with intellectual disabilities: An evaluation of the effectiveness of mindfulness in reducing symptoms of depression and anxiety. *Journal of Intellectual Disability Research, 59,* 93–104. doi:10.1111/jir.12082.

Kabat-Zinn, J. (1990). *Full catastrophe living. Using the wisdom of your body and mind to face stress, pain, and illness*. New York: Dell Publishing.

McGill, P., Papachristoforou, E., & Cooper, V. (2006). Support for family carers of children and young people with developmental disabilities and challenging behaviour. *Child: Care, Health & Development, 32*(2), 159–165.

Neece, C. (2014). Mindfulness-based stress reduction for parents of young children with developmental delays: Implications for parental mental health and child behaviour problems. *Journal of Applied Research in Intellectual Disabilities. 27,* 174–186.

Oono, I. P., Honey, E. J., & McConachie, H. (2013). Parent-mediated early intervention for young children with autism spectrum disorders (ASD). *Evidence-Based Child Health, 8*(6), 2380–2479.

Sakdalan, J. A., Shaw, J., & Collier, V. (2010). Staying in the here-and-now: A pilot study on the use of dialectical behaviour therapy group skills training for forensic clients with intellectual disability. *Journal of Intellectual Disability Research, 54,* 568–572.

Singh, N. N., Wahler, R. G., Adkins, A. D., & Myers, R. E. (2003). Soles of the feet: A mindfulness-based self-control intervention for aggression by an individual with mild mental retardation. *Research in Developmental Disabilities, 24,* 158–169.

Singh, N. N., Lancioni, G. E., Winton, A. S. W., Singh, A. N. A., Adkins, A. D. A., & Singh, J. (2009). Mindful staff can reduce the use of physical restraints when providing care to individuals with intellectual disabilities. *Journal of Applied Research in Intellectual Disabilities, 22,* 194–202.

Singh, N. N., Lancioni, G. E., Singh, A. D. A., Winton, A. S. W., Singh, A. N. A., & Singh, J. (2011). Adolescents with Asperger Syndrome can use a mindfulness-based strategy to control their aggressive behaviour. *Research in Autism Spectrum Disorders, 5,* 1103–1109.

Singh, N., Lancioni, G., Karazsia, B., Winton, A., Myers, R., Singh, A.N.A., & Singh, J. (2013). Mindfulness-based treatment of aggression in individuals with mild intellectual disabilities: A waiting list control study. *Mindfulness, 4,* 158–167.

Singh, N., Lancioni, G., Myers, R., Karazsia, B., Winton, A., & Singh, J. (2014a). A randomised controlled trial of a mindfulness-based smoking cessation program for individuals with mild intellectual disability. *International Journal of Mental Health Addiction. 12,* 153–168.

Singh, N. N., Lancioni, G. E., Winton, A. S. W., Karazsia, B. T., Myers, R. E., Latham, L. I., & Singh, J. (2014b). Mindfulness-based positive behavior support (MBPBS) for mothers of adolescents with autism spectrum disorder: Effects on adolescents' behavior and parental stress. *Mindfulness*. doi:10.1007/s12671-014-0321-3.

Spek, A., van Ham, N., & Nyklicek, I. (2013). Mindfulness-based therapy in adults with an autism spectrum disorder: A randomized controlled trial. *Research in Developmental Disabilities, 34*(1), 246–253.

Stoner, J. B., Bock, S. J., Thompson, J. R., Angell, M. E., Heyl, B. S., & Crowley, E. P. (2005). Welcome to our world: Parent perceptions of interactions between parents of young children with ASD and educational professionals. *Focus on Autism and Other Developmental Disabilities, 20,* 39–51.

Williams, J. M. G., & Kabat-Zinn, J. (2011). Mindfulness: diverse perspectives on its meaning, origins, and multiple applications at the intersection of science and dharma. *Contemporary Buddhism, 12*(1), 1–18.

Chapter 2
A Genealogy of Mindfulness

The concept of mindfulness has its origins in the Sanskrit word *smṛti* and Pāli *sati*, both of which literally mean "memory" (Monier-Williams, 1872; Rhys Davids & Stede, 1999). *Sati* was one of the many technical terms the Buddha developed to map the process of cultivating a healthy mind. In 1881 T. W. Rhys Davids was the first to provide "mindfulness" as an English translation of *sati*, and by 1910, this had become generally accepted (Gethin, 2011). Over the next century mindfulness gradually became absorbed into the English lexicon, first within Theravāda Buddhism and then throughout the wider secular world. In the course of its adoption by Western culture, the *sati* of the Buddha has evolved into the mindfulness that characterises the contemporary mindfulness-based interventions (MBIs) of psychology and related fields.

In this chapter we trace the genealogy of *sati* by first looking at how it is used in the Nikāyas, the early "collections" of the Buddha's teachings, unpacking its meaning and function through the analysis and imagery found there. We will then see how the concept of *sati* has evolved through the twentieth century to become the mindfulness of the contemporary MBIs. This will create a platform for presenting the understanding and application of mindfulness found in the current project as constituting a creative adaptation of this ancient concept, bringing it to individuals and families living with developmental disabilities.

2.1 Sati in the Nikāyas

Mindfulness is the product of an ancient tradition of phenomenology that takes a first-person approach to the systematic analysis of human development and the cultivation of a range of conscious states that are beyond anything normally considered by Western psychology (Grossman, 2010). In order to appreciate the underpinnings of this tradition, it is essential to return to the classical literature that elucidated the concept to generations of scholars and practitioners. This will

Y.-S. Hwang, P. Kearney, *A Mindfulness Intervention for Children with Autism Spectrum Disorder*, Mindfulness in Behavioral Health,
DOI 10.1007/978-3-319-18962-8_2

provide a platform that allows a clear view of the relationship between the classical concept of *sati* and its modern incarnation as mindfulness.

Bhikkhu Bodhi points out that *sati*, while literally meaning memory, "signifies presence of mind, attentiveness to the present, rather than the faculty of memory regarding the past" (Bodhi, 2000b, p. 86). *Sati* as memory does not refer to memory in the ordinary sense of remembering the past; rather, *sati* remembers the present, by keeping the present in mind. We find the same concept presented in the exhortations at railway stations to "mind the gap" when stepping between a train and the platform. Minding the gap here means remembering the act of entering and exiting a train during the actual moment of transit. Mindfulness practice is remembering to stay present. It is the art of not forgetting, and entails tracking both awareness and the object of awareness over time.

When we look at how *sati* is treated in the Nikāyas we find that the establishment of *sati* indicates the beginning of formal meditation practice. In a frequently repeated refrain, the practitioner "sits down, crosses her legs, straightens her back and establishes *sati* directly [*parimukhaṃ satiṃ upaṭṭhapetvā*]"[1] (Mahā-Satipaṭṭhāna Sutta *Larger establishments of mindfulness*, DN 22; Satipaṭṭhāna Sutta *The establishments of mindfulness*, MN 10). The verb associated with *sati* is *upaṭṭhahati*, derived from the prefix *upa*-, denoting nearness or close touch, and the root *sthā*, to stand or station. *Upaṭṭhahati* conveys meanings such as standing near and staying present (Gethin, 2001; Thera, 1969). Rupert Gethin comments:

> The regular Nikāya expression *satiṃ upaṭṭhapetvā* means … "causing mindfulness to stand near," "causing mindfulness to be present" or even "causing mindfulness to come into service." … What is meant … is that *sati* is understood as a quality of mind that "stands near" or "serves" the mind; it watches over the mind. One might say that it is a form of "presence of mind" (Gethin, 2001, p. 32).

The use of the root *sthā* suggests a firm grounding or stationing of the mind, which is elaborated in the metaphors the Buddha uses to speak of *sati*. He compares *sati* to a large post planted firmly in the earth to which a wild elephant is tied. No matter how much he struggles, the elephant cannot escape past the length of rope that ties him to the post, and eventually he gives up his wild behaviour and calms down (Dantabhūmi Sutta *The grade of the tamed*, MN 125).

The function of *sati* is to ground and stabilise the mind. This is further emphasised when the practitioner is described as establishing *sati* "directly", using the adverb *parimukham*. This can be read as "completely (*pari*) facing (*mukha*)" (Rhys Davids & Stede, 1999) the meditation object, establishing a face-to-face encounter with it. Describing the practitioner as "establishing *sati* directly" conveys a firmness and directness in her engagement with the object of experience. This analysis agrees with the understanding of the later Theravāda, where Buddhaghosa (Warren & Kosambi, 1989, XIV, 141), representing the developed orthodoxy, comments that mindfulness appears as confronting an object, like a pillar "firmly planted [*daḷhaṃ patiṭṭhitā*]".

In directly confronting present experience, *sati* calms the senses. The Buddha relates how six wild animals of different species are caught and tied together. The

---

[1] Note that all translations are from the second author, unless otherwise stated.

animals represent the six sense fields (*saḷāyatana*) of seeing, hearing, smelling, tasting, touching and "minding". As with the senses, each animal has its own natural habitat, and they pull in different directions as they strive to return to their familiar territory. At any given moment, the strongest among them dominates (Chappāṇakopama Sutta *Simile of the six animals*, SN 35:247). This image presents the Buddha's understanding of the normal human relationship to sense experience as a perpetual battle between competing drives where the drive that is strongest at any given time wins, until replaced by the next.

Because *sati* is absent or weak, the animals have no central coherence. In contrast, when the six animals are all tied to "a strong pillar or post" then like the elephant their struggle is limited to the length of their rope and eventually they surrender and lie down. The pillar or post here represents mindfulness immersed in body (*kāyagatā sati*).

The Buddha's choice of words and metaphors indicate that *sati* has a grounded, earthy quality and is associated with the project of stabilising and steadying the mind. With this steadiness, *sati* can watch over, guard and protect the mind. For as well as confronting a sense object, *sati* also guards the practitioner like a "gatekeeper" (*dovārika*) (Warren & Kosambi, 1989, XIV, 141), as illustrated in the following discourse.

> Suppose, bhikkhu, a king had a frontier city with strong ramparts, walls and arches, and with six gates. The gatekeeper posted there would be wise, experienced, and intelligent; one who keeps out strangers and admits acquaintances (Kiṃsuka Sutta *The What's-it tree*, SN 35:245).

The Buddha explains that the city is the body, the gatekeeper is *sati*, and the six gates are the six internal sense fields made up of the sensitivities of eye, ear, nose, tongue, body and mind. Awareness or consciousness (*viññāṇa*) is the lord of the city. The city is exposed to, and communicates with, the outside world of the six external sense fields of forms, sounds, odours, tastes, tangibles and phenomena known by the mind. The gatekeeper mediates between the city and the world, checking the flow of traffic as it enters and leaves.

This gatekeeper is described as wise, experienced and intelligent. His job is twofold. First, it is to refuse entrance to the *aññata*, the "unknown", strangers or even enemies. Second, it is to usher in the *ñāta*, the "known", acquaintances, or even friends (Rhys Davids & Stede, 1999). *Sati* here is associated with wisdom, experience and intelligence. *Sati* actively assesses whoever is at the gate, admitting some and refusing others. This assessment entails recognition, or learning from experience over time, for it takes time for *sati* to learn to discern between enemies and friends. It is the steadiness of *sati* that enables it to maintain a continuous watch over the sense gates, and this continuity enables learning to take place. As gatekeeper, *sati* does not simply observe, but observes with discrimination. Discrimination provides the link between *sati* and understanding (*paññā*), and qualities such as recognition and discrimination require an ongoing relationship with the object of experience. This relationship returns us to the role of memory in the functioning of *sati*.

Buddhaghosa (Warren & Kosambi, 1989, XIV, 141) explains *sati* as remembering itself. "By it they remember [*saranti*], or it itself remembers [*sayaṃ sarati*], or it is simply remembering [*saraṇa-mattam*], therefore it is *sati*". Grossman and Van Dam (2011) point out the contrast between seeing mindfulness as process, which is normative for the Buddhist tradition, and that of modern psychology, where mindfulness is seen as a relatively stable trait.

How does it make sense to speak of remembering the present? While we tend to conceive of the present as a moment, perhaps because of our ability to measure time so precisely, the Buddha had a broader, more empirical sense of the present. The present that *sati* remembers is the experienced present, not the momentary present of the clock. For the Buddha, the present is experienced as "change while continuing" (*ṭhitassa aññathatta*) (Ānanda Sutta *To Ānanda*, SN 22.37), a continuously unfolding duration. The present unfolds more as a field than a moment. Although momentary events come and go, the mind remains grounded on the broader activity within which we are currently engaged.

Take as an example mindfulness of driving. We are mindful when we remember *that* we are driving and *how* we are driving. This requires awareness to remain grounded on the act of driving itself. The felt sense of the continuity of driving may include many instances when awareness momentarily slips away, but the mind remembers to return without disruption to the sensed flow of the activity. When we are not mindful, however, when awareness is divided between driving and daydreaming, then we have periods when we forget we are driving and arrive at our destination without any firm memory of what happened during our journey; or we simply get lost. The experience is patchy rather than smooth, discontinuous rather than continuous.

When the Buddha speaks of lapses in mindfulness, the term he uses is "*muṭṭha-sati*", or forgotten mindfulness (Bhayabherava Sutta *Fear and dread*, MN 4). *Muṭṭha* is derived from the verb *mussati*, "to forget", "to pass into oblivion" (Rhys Davids & Stede, 1999), so the opposite of *sati* is oblivion, and specifically the oblivion that comes from forgetting.

For example, if we are packing to go somewhere and rehearsing in our minds what to bring, we are shocked when we arrive and realise that we have forgotten to pack an item we clearly saw and knew we had to bring. What happened? As we rehearsed what we needed to bring with us we experienced a moment of clarity in which we knew we had to pack that particular item, but when awareness moved to the next item the previous one was immediately forgotten. *Sati* was weak, and the object of present experience was quickly forgotten.

Dreyfus (2011, p. 47) follows this line of analysis when he links *sati* to working memory, "the capacity of the mind to maintain and manipulate relevant information so as to be able to engage in purposeful activities". Only when information is retained over time—remembered—can it become understanding. Dreyfus (2011, p. 46) uses a visual perception as an example, explaining that we do not just see discrete "time slices" of an object, but perceive a single person moving from one place to another. Each time slice takes but a moment, while movement from one place to another unfolds through an extended present.

Remembering enables *sati* to monitor experience over time and so guard the senses. This function of *sati* reminds us of its characteristic of groundedness, of being firmly planted on the object. When awareness lands only lightly on an object—as in our example of quickly rehearsing what we need to bring with us—then it leaves no imprint in the mind and is quickly forgotten. When awareness is firmly planted on something, then the object is sufficiently impressed on the mind to allow it to remain available to working memory.

Sati as memory also reveals why the Buddha associated *sati* with wisdom (*paññā*). When we are present to experience over time, when we *remember* present experience, then understanding has the opportunity to arise. The Buddha closely associates *sati* with *sampajañña*, "clear comprehension" (Bodhi, 2000a, p. 2023) or clear understanding, and he often uses the compound term *sati-sampajañña* to convey how similar they are and how closely they work together. Derived from the verb *pajānāti*, "to know", "to understand" (Rhys Davids & Stede, 1999), and the prefix *sam-*, here acting as an intensifier, *sampajañña* conveys the capacity to understand the flow of presently experienced phenomena. This understanding ranges from the basic to the sophisticated. An example of a basic level of *sampajañña* would be how a practitioner practising mindfulness of breathing understands whether or not any given breath is long or short. An example of a sophisticated level would be how the same practitioner understands the workings of the hindrances (*nīvaraṇa*) that characterise an unhealthy mind and the factors of awakening (*bojjhaṅga*) that characterise a healthy mind (Anālayo, 2006). *Sati* remembers to be present, and could be understood as the continuity of presence itself. *Sampajañña* monitors what is remembered as present. *Sampajañña* can be seen as the intelligence implicit in presence, and the compound *sati-sampajañña* could be translated as "intelligent presence".

With this theoretical background, we can approach the two operational definitions of *sati* provided by the Buddha in the Nikāyas. Both are descriptions of practitioners of *sati*. Sekha Sutta (*The trainee*, MN 53) says of the practitioner:

> He has *sati*; possessing supreme *sati* and discrimination [*nepakka*] he can recall and recollect what was done and said long ago.

Here *sati* is linked with memory, along with wisdom in the form of discrimination. *Sati* facilitates memory, in that memory of the past is influenced by the strength of attention to the present. The second definition grounds *sati* on its systematic practice, that of *satipaṭṭhāna*, as outlined in the Satipaṭṭhāna Sutta (*The establishments of mindfulness*, MN 10):

> Here a practitioner, surrendering longing and sorrow for the world, lives tracking body as body, … feeling as feeling … heart-mind as heart-mind … phenomena as phenomena, ardent, clearly understanding and mindful.

This definition takes us to *satipaṭṭhāna*, the practice of mindfulness. The essence of *satipaṭṭhāna* is the practice of tracking experience over time. This practice ties in with *sati* as memory, because tracking something over time requires that we remember to be present to it, maintaining that awareness over time. This understanding ties in with *sati* as guarding the mind, for by maintaining awareness of the flow of experience over time the practitioner learns what aspects of experience should be encouraged and what aspects discouraged. It ties in with wisdom, for when we continuously follow the flow of experienced phenomena we learn to understand them, and the patterns within which they reveal themselves. With this background in mind we can now look at how in the twentieth century the *sati* of the Nikāyas became the mindfulness of the psychologists.

2.2 Mindfulness in the Modern World

We have seen that by 1910 "mindfulness" had become the settled translation of *sati* (Gethin, 2011). The concept was popularised through the work of Nyanaponika Thera (1901–1994), a German scholar monk who was a student of the Burmese meditation master Mahāsī Sayādaw (1904–1982). Nyanaponika Thera worked within the context of the modern Burmese insight movement, a revival of meditation practice that aimed to take meditation out of the monasteries and spread it throughout the general population, in Burma and beyond. This movement began in the mid-nineteenth century and developed throughout the twentieth century, and Mahāsī Sayādaw, U Ba Khin (1899–1971) and S. N. Goenka (1924–2013) were central figures in it. They, along with other teachers, made meditation practice accessible to a mass audience by delivering it through standardised methods that could be practised by ordinary people with the aid of appropriately trained teachers. It could be said that the modern Burmese insight movement democratised Buddhist meditation practice, in that within traditional Buddhist societies it became available to a degree previously unknown, and internationalised it, in that the same methods were applied across cultures (Houtman, 1990, 1999; Jordt, 2007; Kearney, 2011). Textual justification for this understanding of meditation practice was drawn primarily from the Satipaṭṭhāna Sutta (*The establishments of mindfulness*, MN 10), now seen as propounding insight meditation (Gethin, 2011).

Nyanaponika Thera was part of this project of internationalising Buddhist meditation. In his *The heart of Buddhist meditation*, first published in English in 1954, Nyanaponika Thera (1969) presented mindfulness and its practice as the essence of the Buddha's way to liberation, and as available to the general population regardless of whether or not they were Buddhists (Thera, 1969, 1972). He made clear that his purpose was to present mindfulness in its role as right mindfulness, where it functions as an inseparable aspect of the broader system that is the Buddha's noble eightfold path. As such, mindfulness is necessarily accompanied and supported by the other seven path factors, which in practical terms means that, when practised correctly, mindfulness is accompanied and supported by other qualities such as calmness, receptivity and kindness (Thera, 1969). In presenting what he called "satipaṭṭhāna dhamma for all" (Thera, 1969, p. 9), Nyanaponika Thera proclaimed mindfulness practice to be suitable for people of all cultures, including those with no particular religious affiliation. In this he was aligned with the evangelical mission of the modern Burmese insight movement, in its project to laicise and internationalise Buddhist meditation.

Perhaps the aspect of mindfulness that most captured the notice of his readership was his presentation of it as "bare attention", a mode of attention that he claimed strips the mind of its habitual judgements and projections regarding the object of experience (Gethin, 2011; Thera, 1969, 1972). This concept communicates the central aspect of Mahāsī Sayādaw's approach to meditation practice, which is to "note", or be directly and deliberately aware of, any experienced event as simply another meditation object. This includes any thoughts or feelings that arise in relation to the experienced event. These too are just objects to be noted (Mahasi, 1971). As Nyanaponika Thera explained:

> Bare Attention is the clear and single-minded awareness of what actually happens to us and in us, at the successive moments of perception. It is called "bare," because it attends just to the bare facts of a perception as presented either through the five physical senses or through the mind … without reacting to them by deed, speech or by mental comment … If … any such comments arise in one's mind, they themselves are made objects of Bare Attention … (Thera, 1969, p. 30).

This was the understanding of mindfulness that was received and elaborated by newly established meditation teachers such as Joseph Goldstein (1976, 2002) and Jack Kornfield (1993) who were formative influences in the creation of modern North American Buddhism (McMahan, 2008). It was this lineage that shaped Jon Kabat-Zinn's understanding of mindfulness when he developed his new stress reduction programme in the late 1970s (Gethin, 2011; Kabat-Zinn, 2011). Kabat-Zinn borrowed directly from Nyanaponika Thera when he referred to mindfulness as "the heart of Buddhist meditation" (Kabat-Zinn, 1990, p. 12), and his project to bring mindfulness to a secular, non-Buddhist audience was the same as that of Nyanaponika Thera and the modern Burmese insight movement.

When Nyanaponika Thera explained mindfulness as a path factor, necessarily accompanied and supported by other path factors, he drew upon his traditional understanding of the Buddha's theoretical framework, that of dependent arising (Kalupahana, 1975). In this paradigm, reality is analysed in terms of experienced events rather than of entities, events that arise, function and cease in dependence upon other experienced events. As in Buddhaghosa's analysis of mindfulness above, what appear to be stable, independently existing things turn out, upon analysis, to be dynamic processes. The events that emerge from these processes are distinguished from each other through their characteristics and the conditional relationships that give rise to them. For mindfulness to be mindfulness, therefore, it must have certain characteristics that distinguish it from other phenomena, *and* it must be embedded within a particular network of relationships with these other phenomena. Mindfulness, like other phenomena within this network, is never alone. One could even say that mindfulness alone does not exist; it exists only as part of a broader phenomenal network.

As the practice of mindfulness transitioned to modern, secular contexts, the original theoretical context of its practice transitioned into new ways of understanding it, where mindfulness was not so much seen as accompanied and conditioned by other qualities such as kindness and receptivity but as *containing* these other qualities. Mindfulness could be seen as standing alone, as the container of the different qualities traditionally associated with it. In brief, mindfulness has tended to become a collective rather than a unitary term.

We can see this shift illustrated in a representative definition of mindfulness as understood in the context of the contemporary MBIs. Kabat-Zinn has defined mindfulness as "the awareness that emerges through paying attention on purpose, in the present moment, and nonjudgmentally to the unfolding of experience moment by moment" (Kabat-Zinn, 2003, p. 145). This definition presents mindfulness as a collective term that entails at least four aspects, those of awareness, attention, intentionality and a particular kind of attitude. In this understanding mindfulness is not associated with these phenomena, but contains them.

The significance of this distinction will be outlined below, as we survey how mindfulness has entered into the contemporary MBIs. We will begin with Mindfulness-Based Stress Reduction (MBSR), the program that could be seen as transitioning the understanding of *sati* mediated by the modern insight movement into the social sciences, and from there look at Mindfulness-Based Cognitive Therapy (MBCT), Acceptance and Commitment Therapy (ACT) and Dialectical Behavior Therapy (DBT).

2.3 Mindfulness-Based Stress Reduction

MBSR is perhaps the most influential mindfulness-based programme in the contemporary world, and it continues to provide a model for other mindfulness-based interventions. In the 1970s its founder, Jon Kabat-Zinn, was a practitioner of Korean Seon Buddhism and Theravāda mindfulness meditation as taught at the Insight Meditation Society (IMS) in Barre Massachusetts, who also practised and taught yoga (Kabat-Zinn, 2003). During a meditation retreat in 1979 he was inspired to share what he had learnt of these practices to people who would ordinarily never enter a yoga or meditation centre (Kabat-Zinn, 2011). He created a Stress Reduction Clinic at the University of Massachusetts Medical Center to teach mindfulness meditation to medical patients who were not being adequately served by conventional treatments. Given the scientific and secular context within which he was operating, he felt he needed to strip meditation of "the cultural, religious, and ideological factors associated with the Buddhist origins of mindfulness" (Kabat-Zinn, 2003, p. 149). If this approach was successful, mindfulness meditation could then be extended to a range of other settings (Kabat-Zinn, 2003).

How can mindfulness practice be divorced from its Buddhist origins yet remain authentic in its expression? Like other teachers in North American Buddhism, Kabat-Zinn located his understanding of mindfulness in the traditional Indian concept of "dharma" as the expression of a universal truth that transcends traditional religious boundaries (e.g. Kornfield, 1993). This approach drew upon Nyanaponika Thera's aspiration that "satipaṭṭhāna dhamma for all" would ultimately spread beyond the boundaries of Buddhism itself (Thera, 1969, p. 9), which in turn was characteristic of the modern Burmese insight movement. This turn towards mindfulness meditation as the expression of a universalist ethos, therefore, can be traced back to at least the mid-nineteenth century.

Needing a distinctive brand name for his program, Kabat-Zinn settled upon Mindfulness-Based Stress Reduction (Kabat-Zinn, 2011), where he used "mindfulness" as a concept that could function as "an umbrella term broad enough to contain the multiplicity of key elements that seems essential to field a successful clinical programme" (Kabat-Zinn, 2011, p. 288). The programme itself was carefully constructed on a practice of sitting and walking meditation supported by yoga. Meditation techniques included mindfulness of breathing and body scan, or systematically scanning the body with awareness (Kabat-Zinn, 1990). This style of meditation practice is easily recognisable as essentially the same as that taught in the contemporary American insight movement (e.g., Goldstein, 1976).

In presenting mindfulness and its practice, Kabat-Zinn provided both an operational definition of how mindfulness worked, around which he organised the practical instructions he gave to his patients, and a broader theoretical framework or paradigm (1990, pp. 149–50) that could show what mindfulness was and how it fitted into a coherent view of the world.

We have already seen one representative definition of mindfulness practice that Kabat-Zinn provided as "the awareness that emerges through paying attention on purpose, in the present moment, and nonjudgmentally to the unfolding of experience moment by moment" (2003, p. 145). We have noted that this is an operational definition that presents mindfulness as a collective term containing within it at least four aspects, those of awareness, attention, intentionality and a particular kind of attitude. This definition provides both the "what" and the "how" of mindfulness. The "what" aspect provides the identity of mindfulness, while the "how" provides its function. Here, the identity of mindfulness is the awareness that emerges from a specific process, and its function is the cultivation of purposive attention to the unfolding of experience, in the present, and without judgement.

We have seen that the Buddha took a similar approach in his operational definitions of mindfulness. One difference to be noted is the slide in Kabat-Zinn's definition from seeing mindfulness as a unitary term supported by other qualities to a collective term containing other qualities. Another distinction is that the Buddha is even less concerned with identity and more concerned with function. In his satipaṭṭhāna definition cited above, the Buddha simply describes how mindfulness is practised: "surrendering longing and sorrow for the world, [the practitioner] lives tracking body as body, … feeling as feeling … heart-mind as heart-mind … phenomena as phenomena, ardent, clearly understanding and mindful" (Satipaṭṭhāna Sutta *The establishments of mindfulness*, DN 22 & MN 10). Here, mindfulness is defined as a practice of tracking experience over time in a certain way (conveyed by "body *as* body … heart-mind *as* heart-mind"), supported by ardency, clear understanding and mindfulness itself. In the satipaṭṭhāna definition, mindfulness remains a unitary construct within a more general practice, although the Buddha here does not attempt to define that construct. When Buddhaghosa focuses on the nature of mindfulness itself, he also emphasises function over identity when he defines mindfulness as "simply remembering" (Warren and Kosambi, 1989, XIV, 141). Mindfulness, which as we have seen literally means memory, is the activity of "simply remembering". For the Buddha and the tradition he founded, identity ultimately *is* function.

All these operational definitions are embedded within and receive their meaning from a theoretical framework; and in all these examples, the framework is dharma. In constructing his own presentation of dharma, Kabat-Zinn could draw upon the universalism and eclecticism that already characterised North American Buddhism (McMahan, 2008). He presented dharma as a universal grammar that provides a phenomenological analysis of the nature of human experience (Kabat-Zinn, 2003). He saw wholeness and connectedness as fundamental to understanding the workings of the body and mind, and even the universe itself, and drew upon both science and traditional forms of Buddhist and non-Buddhist dharma as his authorities (Kabat-Zinn, 1990). All this constituted an attempt to allow the theoretical framework of mindfulness to fit into a secular context so it could be accepted by a wide variety of people without conflicting with the ideological commitments they already possessed.

2.4 Mindfulness-Based Cognitive Therapy

Segal, Williams and Teasdale (2002) mark the beginnings of cognitive therapy in the work of Aaron T. Beck in the 1960s and 1970s. It had been commonly assumed that negative thinking characterising depression was only an effect of an underlying cause and not itself a cause of depression, and Beck realised this assumption is wrong; negative thinking is as much a cause as an effect. He therefore encouraged his patients to become aware of their patterns of thinking. Segal et al. (2002) subsequently concluded that what was central in this process of cultivating awareness of one's thinking was not the content of negative thoughts, but one's relationship to these thoughts. It was therefore important to change the relationship patients had to negative thoughts and feelings, so they could learn to see them as simply "passing events in the mind that were neither necessarily valid reflections of reality nor central aspects of the self" (p. 38).

This bears a marked similarity with the Buddha's understanding of the causal nature of the relationships between thoughts and feelings (e.g. Madhupiṇḍika Sutta *The sweet essence*, MN18) and the importance of the practice of mindfulness of thoughts and feelings. It is therefore not surprising that when Segal, Williams and Teasdale discovered Jon Kabat-Zinn's mindfulness programme, they quickly appreciated how useful it could be as a pragmatic tool in their own work, to reveal the psychological patterns they wanted their patients to appreciate.

Since this kind of practice was unknown in cognitive therapy, Segal et al. (2002) simply adopted Kabat-Zinn's operational definition of mindfulness along with the theoretical framework within which it was embedded. For example, Segal et al. (2002) borrowed Kabat-Zinn's distinction between "doing mode" and "being mode". Mindfulness allows patients "to become more aware of their mode of mind ('mental gear') at any moment, and the skills to disengage, if they choose, from unhelpful modes of mind and to engage more helpful modes" (Segal et al., 2002, p. 70). Doing mode, characterised by a struggle to escape habitual negative patterns of mind and emotions through obsessive thinking, is unhelpful. Being mode, characterised by accepting present circumstances and experiencing them directly, without filtering them through thoughts of evaluation and possible outcomes, is helpful. When thoughts and feelings are not perceived as independent and enduring realities, but as passing events that arise, are recognised and then vanish, automatic responses are not triggered and a sense of freedom emerges. Mindfulness is the essential first step in this process of "decentring" (Segal et al., 2002, p. 74), which is central to this therapy.

Here we see a direct transmission of a practice and its theoretical framework from MBSR to MBCT, with appropriate modifications being made to adapt the mindfulness practice to the population to which MBCT is directed. Hence the focus on using mindfulness to enable patients to understand the underlying mental patterns associated with their depression. Looked at from the other side, we could say that Cognitive Therapy had already developed its own dharma, a systematic understanding of the nature of reality (Gethin, 1998), within which they had come to an appreciation of the dynamic relationships between thought and emotion, and an understanding that some kind of attention training, one that would expose these relationships to their patients, would be extremely useful. Simply by following the trajectory of their own dharma, Segal, Williams and Teasdale came to appreciate the need for some kind of attention training, which they found in the mindfulness meditation practised in MBSR. All they needed was the technical information regarding how to practise and teach it, and some modification of their own theoretical framework—their dharma—within which its practice and pedagogy could be wrapped.

2.5 Acceptance and Commitment Therapy

The theoretical foundation of ACT is provided by functional contextualism, a philosophy of science characterised by a pragmatic theory of truth where a statement is regarded as "true" if it facilitates desired consequences—if it "works"—rather than if it points to a corresponding state of the world. The practical consequences of such a philosophy include an interest in the nature of our beliefs and our relationships to them along with a particular focus on the consequences of our actions. ACT is also concerned with the unique role that language, in the deeper sense of symbolic activity, plays in stimulating human suffering. Suffering occurs when we mistake the symbolic representations within our minds for literal reality, when we live within the stories of our lives, thinking our stories *about* reality are actually reality (Hayes, Strosahl, & Wilson, 2012). The journey out of this entanglement lies through the cultivation of psychological flexibility, and mindfulness practice constitutes a major support for developing psychological flexibility (Hayes et al., 2012) .

From this perspective, much human suffering comes from attachment to the contents of the mind—thoughts and emotions—that cause people to over-identify, or "fuse", with them. Mindfulness allows the client to disidentify with these mental contents, allowing them to come and go freely. The counterpart to this practice is to learn to locate one's identity in the "observer perspective" from which these mental events are seen (Hayes et al., 2012, p. 66), rather than from within the contents of the stories created by the mind.

We can see here how, as with MBCT, the creators of ACT developed a dharma, a systematic understanding of the nature of the mind and its relationships, through the logic of their social scientific study. They came to appreciate the usefulness of mindfulness practice, without any prior reference to Buddhism, when it became clear that developing the capacity to attend skilfully to one's inner world would have therapeutic benefits. As with MBCT, ACT lacked a practical methodology of attention training already at hand that they could draw upon to actualise the theory they had developed. This practice needed to be borrowed from outside their tradition. In contrast with MBCT, however, ACT did not draw from the philosophy of MBSR to contextualise the practice of mindfulness, for its creators already had their own theoretical framework in place.

Despite having been developed independently of the Buddha's teaching, ACT's philosophy contains some interesting parallels to it. For example, ACT's avoidance of ontological commitments in favour of a practical study of the consequences of actions echoes the Buddha (Gowans, 2003). Also, the ACT concept of flexible attention as an essential aspect of psychological flexibility is very similar to the Buddha's concept of *yoniso manasikāra*, "careful attention" (Bodhi, 2012) or "appropriate attention" (Thanissaro, 1996), and its role in uncovering delusion.

Given these similarities, it is not surprising that mindfulness has found a role within ACT. However, the creators of ACT appear to see mindfulness as useful solely in terms of its contribution to attention training. They show no interest in its origins and traditional theoretical framework, presumably because ACT already has a developed philosophy behind it. This makes for an interesting distinction with MBSR in the way mindfulness practice is regarded. Kabat-Zinn, for example, is firm on the necessity to avoid tampering in any way with the particular bundle of practices that make up MBSR (McCown, Reibel, & Micozzi, 2011). This makes sense, given that MBSR is defined primarily around its practices rather than its philosophy. Change the practice and MBSR itself is changed, while the practice of MBSR can be compatible with different streams of theoretical interpretation, as illustrated by the shifts in Kabat-Zinn's own writings and in the freedom MBSR instructors have in developing their own styles of theory (e.g., McCown et al., 2011). ACT, in contrast, is defined around its theoretical framework to the degree that its creators have declared that "any method based on the psychological flexibility theory we have described here could be called 'ACT' if those employing the methods choose to describe it in that way (Hayes et al., 2012, p. 97)". With ACT, change the theory and ACT is changed, while mindfulness practice may or may not be added, depending on its clinical usefulness in any given context.

2.6 Dialectical Behavior Therapy

The theoretical framework of DBT is based on dialectics, which functions both as a worldview and as a form of therapeutic relationship aimed at a particular clinical population, those with Borderline Personality Disorder. Dialectics is characterised by a system, conception of reality, an understanding that reality is not static but is comprised of different and opposing forces in constant change, such that reality itself is found in process rather than content, change rather than structure (Linehan, 1993a, b). This systems approach assumes an understanding of causation that rejects simple linear causal chains in favour of a more complex and dynamic causal network (Linehan, 1993a).

Dialectics influences therapy through a particular form of dialogue with patients in which no conclusion is taken as final (Linehan, 1993a). Patients learn to hold contradictory positions within the context of a broader dialectical space, without becoming fixed on either. Linehan gives the example of simultaneously holding the positions of "I want to live" and "I want to die" (1993a, p. 35). Patients are also trained in a number of skill sets, those of mindfulness (regarded as a core skill that underlies the others), interpersonal effectiveness, emotion regulation and distress tolerance (Linehan, 1993b).

Mindfulness in DBT is defined in terms of "what" and "how" skills, or identity and function. The "what" skills are "learning to observe, to describe, and to participate", and the "how" skills are "taking a nonjudgmental stance, focusing on one thing in the moment, being effective" (Linehan, 1993a, p. 144). This conception is very close to that found in MBSR. Mindfulness training focuses on cultivating the capacity to be aware of one's emotions as they come and go, the behaviours that are stimulated from them, and the dialectical relationships between them.

The underlying philosophy of DBT is sophisticated, naturalistic, empirical and utilitarian. In this and in other ways, it shares clear similarities with the Buddha's dharma. For example, the understanding of causation in DBT is similar to that of the Buddha's doctrine of dependent arising (*paṭiccasamuppāda*), and the dialectical balance, for example that between the desire to live and the desire to die, resembles the Buddha's middle way (*majjhima paṭipadā*). It is therefore not surprising that mindfulness practice fits neatly into this philosophy. As with the other MBIs, however, DBT lacks its own method of attention training and had to borrow it from outside. In this case, given Marsha Linehan's own background in Zen, mindfulness practice was borrowed from Buddhism, and Zen in particular (1993a, b).

2.7 The Problem of Secularisation

Our survey of the genealogy of mindfulness has touched upon issues of cross-fertilisation across traditions, in particular how contemporary therapies have turned to mindfulness practice as a way of adapting a traditional form of attention training to enable their participants to cultivate fluency in the workings of their own minds. Different therapies have developed different relationships to mindfulness practice, but underlying all of them is what could be called the problem of secularisation.

When Kabat-Zinn developed a programme that would bring the benefits of Buddhist meditation to a wider, secular audience, he felt the need to remove it from its oriental and religious origins. Facing the same situation, Marsha Linehan advised her DBT trainers:

> Sometimes individuals will be put off by references to Eastern meditation practices. You need to be very sensitive to this point. You can either divorce meditation from any religion or relate it to all religions (Linehan, 1993b, p. 65).

Although this approach may allow patients to engage mindfulness practice without challenging their pre-existing beliefs, it is inadequate in the context of the scientific study of mindfulness practice and its effects because it sidesteps the issue of the nature of mindfulness and its practice.

To suggest a way out from this difficulty we might begin by pointing out that the very project of seeing the adaptation of mindfulness practice as one entailing a conflict between religion and secularism presupposes the imposition of a European cultural category onto a situation where such categories are not necessarily useful. The very idea of "religion" as being in opposition to "philosophy" and "science" is an invention of European thought (King, 1999). The Buddha taught dharma, and dharma is an Indian cultural category that does not correspond with any European cultural category, whether religion, psychology or philosophy. However, dharma as the Buddha taught it does have significant family resemblances to all three of these projects, and it has been presented as each of them, depending on the audience appealed to (Gowans, 2003; McMahan, 2008).

Dharma, in the sense in which the Buddha uses the term, is an empirical, naturalistic project that avoids any unnecessary ontological commitments in favour of the practical task of easing human suffering (Kalupahana, 1992). If we were looking for contemporary examples of dharma in the sense that the Buddha uses it, we could find them among the MBIs we have been examining.

MBCT, for example, aims to allow patients to understand and work with the mental processes that give rise to and maintain depression, and this requires cultivating an understanding of the workings of the mind in general. MBCT employs a model of the mind that encompasses both health and morbidity, and uses mindfulness to allow patients to "become more aware of their mode of mind ('mental gear') at any moment, and the skills to disengage, if they choose, from unhelpful modes of mind and to engage more helpful modes" (Segal et al., 2002, p. 70). This is isomorphic with the Buddha's underlying ethical principle, that of cultivating the wholesome (*kusala*) and abandoning the unwholesome (*akusala*) in order to facilitate human flourishing (Harvey, 2000).

ACT therapists share this pragmatic emphasis by focusing on the consequences of their clients' actions, and how these consequences align with their values and purposes. Clients are encouraged to identify and cultivate actions that are in accordance with their deeply held values and abandon actions that violate those values. Mindfulness practice enables them to let go of identification with the contents of their minds so that they are not led into activities that result in greater suffering (Hayes et al., 2012). Finally, DBT draws upon a dialectical view that emphasises the complexity and ubiquity of causation and change, and within this framework trains patients to modulate their emotions, abandon maladaptive behaviours and cultivate behaviours that enhance their quality of life (Linehan, 1993a).

These three systems hold certain characteristics in common. Each represents a naturalistic explanation of how human beings create suffering for themselves and how they may work their way out of this suffering into a more satisfactory and authentic life. This practical project is based on a theoretical understanding of the workings of the mind and of the perceptions the mind creates. Theory needs to be put into practice, and one essential element of this practice is what could be called a technology of attention, a systematic way of training attention to allow the individual to directly perceive the processes that are the subject of theoretical explanation.

The Buddha's dharma shares the same characteristics. It too has a sophisticated model of causation/conditionality (*paṭiccasamuppāda*) that underlies its practical concerns, a model that requires no divine intervention to function. Like the MBIs, the Buddha is concerned with the consequences of behaviour, and he classifies actions in terms of their consequences. That which is "wrong" (*pāpa*) or "unwholesome" (*akusala*) is that which gives rise to results that add to the suffering of oneself and others, while that which is "wholesome" (*kusala*) is that which gives rise to results that reduce the suffering of oneself and others (Harvey, 2000; Keown, 2001).

One characteristic that distinguishes the Buddha's dharma from the contemporary MBIs is that alongside its theoretical framework, it also developed its own sophisticated system for training attention in order to study and understand the workings of the mind. This practical craft of attention training has been named "mindfulness" in contemporary psychology. When mindfulness was originally borrowed from the Buddha's dharma, the adaptation was driven, in part, by a sense that mindfulness practice had to be distanced from its origins, because of the "religious" nature of those origins. However, once we distinguish the Buddha's dharma from the later variety of Buddhisms that emerged from it (Robinson, Johnson, & Ṭhānissaro 2005), we open up the possibility of treating this dharma as a purely secular enterprise that can be unpacked to reveal more of the practical craft information concerning meditation practice that it possesses, along with any relevant insights from its secular approach to ethics and its understanding of the nature of an authentic human life.

2.8 Our Approach

This brings us to the approach that we bring to the contemporary discourse of mindfulness. As we have seen, the *sati* of the Buddha is not identical to the mindfulness of contemporary psychology—which is why thus far we have been careful to keep the two terms separate. Contemporary mindfulness is a direct descendant of the Buddha's *sati*, but it has as many differences as similarities to its ancestor. For example, while *sati* is a unitary term, mindfulness is collective. Also, the Buddha's *sati* comes to us already contained within a sophisticated theoretical framework—a dharma—that sees it as one part of a complex whole, while mindfulness can be used as a floating signifier that can mean different things in different contexts. However, if mindfulness practice is to become firmly established within a secular, scientific context then it needs to look to both its theoretical foundations and its practical methodology. Otherwise, it will be in danger of withering over time.

In the following chapters, we will present one attempt to ground the practice of mindfulness in the framework provided by the Buddha himself, in a way that is entirely compatible with contemporary scientific and secular concerns. We will apply the practice of mindfulness to a population of six mothers of children with ASD and aggressive behaviours, and to the children themselves. Our theoretical framework is grounded directly in the work of the Buddha, treating him not as the founder of a religion but as a theoretical and practical psychologist, while at the same time we attempt to follow the example of Jon Kabat-Zinn by making the practical adaptations necessary to allow this particular population to practise mindfulness meditation and gain the maximum benefits from their practice.

References

Anālayo. (2006). *Satipatthana: The direct path to realization*. Birmingham: Windhorse Publications.

Bodhi, B. (2000a). *The connected discourses of Buddha: A translation of the Samyutta Nikaya*. Boston: Wisdom Publications.

Bodhi, B. (Ed.). (2000b). *Abhidhammattha sangaha. A comprehensive manual of abhidhamma*. Seattle: BPS Pariyatti

Bodhi, B. (2012). *The numerical discourses of the Buddha: A translation of the Anguttara Nikaya*. Boston: Wisdom Publications.

Dreyfus, G. (2011). Is mindfulness present-centred and non-judgmental? A discussion of the cognitive dimensions of mindfulness. *Contemporary Buddhism, 12*(1), 41–54.

Gethin, R. (1998). *The foundations of Buddhism*. Oxford: Oxford University Press.

Gethin, R. (2001). *The Buddhist path to awakening: A study of the bodhi-pakkhiyā-dhammā*. Oxford: Oneworld Publications.

Gethin, R. (2011). On some definitions of mindfulness. *Contemporary Buddhism, 12*(1), 263–279.

Goldstein, J. (1976). *The experience of insight. A natural unfolding*. Santa Cruz: Unity Press.

Goldstein, J. (2002). *One dharma: The emerging western Buddhism*. London: Rider.

Gowans, C. W. (2003). *Philosophy of the Buddha*. London: Routledge.

Grossman, P. (2010). Mindfulness for psychologists: Paying kind attention to the perceptible. *Mindfulness, 1*, 87–97.

Grossman, P., & Van Dam, N. T. (2011). Mindfulness, by any other name …: Trials and tribulations of sati in western psychology and science. *Contemporary Buddhism, 12*(1), 219–239.

Harvey, P. (2000). *An introduction to Buddhist ethics. Foundations, values & issues*. Cambridge: Cambridge University Press.

Hayes, S., Strosahl, K. D., & Wilson, K. G. (2012). *Acceptance and commitment therapy: The process and practice of mindful change* (2nd ed.). New York: Guilford.

Houtman, G. (1990). *Traditions of Buddhist practice in Burma*. London University. https://http://www.academia.edu/1836315/. (Burmese Traditions of Buddhist Practice).

Houtman, G. (1999). *Mental Culture in Burmese Crisis Politics* Monograph Series. https://http://www.academia.edu/1836314/. (Mental Culture in Burmese Crisis Politics Aung San Suu Kyi and the National League for Democracy).

Jordt, I. (2007). *Burma's mass lay meditation movement: Buddhism and the cultural construction of power*. Athens: Ohio University Press.

Kabat-Zinn, J. (1990). *Full catastrophe living. Using the wisdom of your body and mind to face stress, pain, and illness*. New York: Dell Publishing.

Kabat-Zinn, J. (2003). Mindfulness-based interventions in context: Past, present, and future. *Clinical psychology: Science and Practice, 10*, 144–156.

Kabat-Zinn, J. (2011). Some reflections on the origins of MBSR, skillful menas, and the trouble with maps. *Contemporary Buddhism, 12*(1), 281–306.

Kalupahana, D. J. (1975). *Causality: The central philosophy of Buddhism*. Honolulu: University Press of Hawaii.

Kalupahana, D. J. (1992). *A history of Buddhist philosophy. Continuities & discontinuities*. Honolulu: University of Hawaii Press.

Kearney, P. (2011). Transformations of insight. In C. Rocha & M. Barker (Eds.), *Buddhism in Australia: Traditions in change* (pp. 107–112). Abingdon: Routledge.

Keown, D. (2001). *The nature of Buddhist ethics*. Basingstroke: Palgrave.

King, R. (1999). *Orientalism and religion: Postcolonial theory, India and "The Mystic East"*. London: Routeldge.

Kornfield, J. (1993). *A path with heart: A guide through the perils and promises of spiritual life*. New York: Bantam.

Linehan, M. M. (1993a). *Cognitive-behavioural treatment of borderline personality disorder*. New York: Guilford.

Linehan, M. M. (1993b). *Skills training manual for treating borderline personality disorder*. New York: Guilford.

Mahasi. (1971). *Practical insight meditation. Basic and progressive stages*. Kandy: Buddhist Publication Society.

McCown, D., Reibel, D., & Micozzi, M. S. (2011). *Teaching minduflness: A practical guide for clinicians and educators*. New York: Springer.

McMahan, D. L. (2008). *The making of Buddhist modernism*. Oxford: Oxford University Press.

Monier-Williams, M. (1872). *Sanskrit-English dictionary etymologically and philologically arranged*. Oxford: Clarendon Press.

Rhys Davids, T. W., & Stede, W. (Eds.). (1999). *The Pali Text Society's Pali-English dictionary*. Oxford: The Pali Text Society.

Robinson, R. H., Johnson, W. L., & Ṭhānissaro, B. (2005). *Buddhist religions. A historical introduction*. Belmont: Wadsworth/Thomson Learning.

Segal, Z. V., Williams, J. M. G., & Teasdale, J. D. (2002). *Mindfulness-based cognitive therapy for depression: A new approach to preventing relapse*. New York: Guilford.

Thanissaro. (1996). *The wings to awakening. An anthology from the Pali Canon*. Massachusetts: Dhamma Dana Publications.

Thera, N. (1969). *The heart of Buddhist meditation*. London: Rider & Company.

Thera, N. (1972). *The power of mindfulness*. San Francisco: Unity Press.

Warren, H. C., & Kosambi, D. (Eds.). (1989). *Visuddhimagga of Buddhaghosācariya*. Delhi: Motilal Banarsidass.

References

Chapter 3
Mindfulness and Disability

In recent decades the *sati* of the Buddha has transmuted into the mindfulness of contemporary psychology and related fields, and has become a valuable instrument in the treatment of a variety of clinical populations. Recently, mindfulness has also been applied to the behavioural and psychological difficulties of individuals with developmental disabilities (DD) (Hwang & Kearney, 2013). DD comprise a range of conditions that arise from impairments occurring during the developmental period in physical, learning, language, or behaviour areas (Centers for Disease Control and Prevention, 2013). Usually life-long, these conditions have the potential to limit a person's everyday functioning. DD include autism spectrum disorder (ASD) and intellectual disabilities (ID), both of which are of particular interest to this study.

This chapter presents a systematic review of mindfulness interventions for people living with DD, with a particular focus on ASD and ID. This review is undertaken to establish what has already been accomplished in the application of mindfulness to this population, to identify the strengths of current mindfulness interventions and the areas for their possible improvement in the future. The review covers the objectives, content, method and outcomes of these interventions, with particular attention to the ways in which mindfulness has been taught and practised. The chapter then compares mindfulness interventions with those that address similar behavioural and psychological issues without using mindfulness, in an attempt to establish what gives mindfulness interventions their distinctive character. Prior to the review we will briefly look into the issues that people living with DD are reported to encounter.

3.1 Developmental Disabilities

While the prevalence rates for DD are mixed overall, those for ASD are increasing (CDC, 2012). ASD is characterised by impairments in social communication and social interaction, along with restricted repetitive patterns of behaviours, interests or activities (American Psychiatric Association, 2013). When a recent US National Health Interview Survey found a 17% increase in DD over 1997–2008, it was due

Y.-S. Hwang, P. Kearney, *A Mindfulness Intervention for Children with Autism Spectrum Disorder*, Mindfulness in Behavioral Health,
DOI 10.1007/978-3-319-18962-8_3

largely to increases in the prevalence of ASD (Boyle et al., 2011). In Australia, data from the Australian Bureau of Statistics (ABS, 2012) show that between 2003 and 2009 the prevalence of DD decreased among the 0–14 years age cohort, but the prevalence of ASD increased from 6.2 to 13 %. ASD is also frequently associated with ID. In the USA, for example, about 24 % of individuals with ASD have IQs in the range 71–85, and 38 % have IQs below 70 (CDC, 2012).

Individuals with DD, including ASD and ID, are at increased risk of developing behavioural problems (Kolaitis, 2008; Richard Hastings, 2002) and mental health problems (Emerson, 2003; Mazzucchelli & Sanders, 2011). They are two to three times more likely to develop behavioural and mental health problems than those without DD (de Ruiter, Dekker, Verhulst, & Koot, 2007). These problems are not mutually exclusive. Individuals with DD who have severe behavioural problems are more likely to present with psychiatric disorders (Grey, Pollard, McClean, MacAuley, & Hastings, 2010). This confluence of behavioural and psychological problems calls for timely investigation into possible solutions.

The difficulties faced by individuals with DD also influence their families and carers. Parents of individuals with DD, for example, undergo elevated parenting stress, and this is especially so in families living with individuals with ASD. Parents of children with ASD have been found to experience twice the stress of parents of children with other types of DD and four times that of parents whose children who do not have any DD (Silva & Schalock, 2012). These elevated stress levels have the potential to induce family crises (Weiss & Lunsky, 2011). Care providers of individuals with DD also tend to suffer stress and burnout, adversely affecting their relationships with those for whom they are caring (Hastings, 2002), which in turn increases the likelihood for challenging behaviour from their care recipients (Hastings, 2005; McGrath, 2013) .

Research into families living with individuals with DD indicates that the relationships between children with problem behaviour and parents undergoing stress are transactional in nature (Neece, Green, & Baker, 2012), as are the relationships between individuals with DD and their professional carers (Hastings & Brown, 2002). This leads to the possibility that if the problems are transactional in nature, then so also may be their solutions. Several recent studies have used a transactional approach in applying mindfulness to these issues and have had some success in reducing behavioural problems in people with DD and increasing the psychological well-being of their care providers (e.g. Singh et al., 2009, 2010). The following sections focus on mindfulness interventions that have been provided for individuals with DD and their care providers, focusing in particular on people living with ASD and ID.

3.2 Studies in Mindfulness and Developmental Disabilities

We have published two systematic literature reviews regarding intervention studies that teach mindfulness to individuals with DD and their care providers, where the first paper concerned individuals with DD (Hwang & Kearney, 2013) and the second their care providers (Hwang & Kearney, 2014). The first paper showed the importance of long-term practice for individuals with DD if they are to gain any long-lasting beneficial results from their mindfulness training. The second paper demonstrated that mindfulness practice both benefits the care providers of individuals with DD and can improve the level of care they provide. In turn, individuals with DD who are under the care of mindfulness practitioners enjoy benefits such as reductions in their aggressive behaviours that illustrate the transactional nature of the relationships between care providers and their care recipients. Taken together, these two papers indicated that the results of mindfulness interventions could be classified as either direct or indirect, depending on whether the benefits of mindfulness practice on the practitioners themselves are considered or the benefits that accrue to those under their care.

To continue our exploration of both the direct and indirect effects of mindfulness training we conducted a follow-up systematic review of intervention studies published since April 2012, which was the cut-off date for our previous review. We had two questions in mind: (1) What happens to individuals with DD when they practise mindfulness? and (2) What happens to individuals with DD when their family and professional care providers practise mindfulness? The second question was designed to examine the transactional nature of the relationships between care providers and recipients. The procedures and criteria of the earlier review were applied (Hwang & Kearney, 2013, 2014) but with the addition of a new criterion, the indirect effects of mindfulness practice on care recipients in studies that train family or professional care providers in mindfulness. This review process identified eight studies that taught mindfulness to individuals with DD and met the new criterion (Table 3.1). A hand search (e.g. references) revealed a further six relevant studies, two for individuals with DD and four for care providers of individuals with DD.

We then revisited the mindfulness intervention studies used in the original reviews (Hwang & Kearney, 2013, 2014). Of the 19 studies, two did not meet the new criterion and were excluded. The current review therefore includes 31 mindfulness intervention studies, 17 from the original reviews and 14 that were recently identified. Of these, 21 are studies of individuals with DD and seven are studies of care providers of individuals with DD, three of which trained both care providers and care recipients with DD.

The updated review identifies three mindfulness-based approaches that have been used to support individuals with DD:

- Intervention studies that directly support individuals with DD by training them in mindfulness (category 1 interventions).
- Intervention studies that indirectly support individuals with DD by training their family or professional care providers in mindfulness (category 2 interventions).
- Intervention studies that support individuals with DD both directly and indirectly by providing mindfulness interventions to both those with DD and their care providers (category 3 interventions).

Table 3.1 Results of search strategy (published 2012–2014)

Combination of keywords	ProQuest	PsycINFO	Web of Science	Medline	Scopus	Step 1 Duplicated references	Step 2 Not meet criteria 1–3 (Abstract)	Step 2 Meet criteria 1–3 (Abstract)	Step 2 Meet criteria 1–3 (Full text)	Step 3
Mindfulness and disabilit*	29	10	3	1	10	53->41	28	13	11	6
Mindfulness and autis*	5	4	1	2	3	15->6	5	1	1	1
Mindfulness and asperger*	0	0	1	1	1	3->0	0			
Mindfulness and impairment	0	1	1	0	1	3->1 Total 48	0 Total 33	1 Total 15	1 Total 13	1 Total 8
Duplicated references	1	2	1	2	3	–	–	–	–	–

Note: An asterisk was used to broaden the search. For example, disabilit* was used to include publications, which utilised the word, disability and disabilities.

3.2.1 *Mindful Learning: Training Individuals with DD in Mindfulness*

Category 1 interventions provided mindfulness training to the individuals with DD themselves and examined its direct effects. This is the largest category, containing 21 of the 31 intervention studies. These studies are analysed according to mindfulness practitioner characteristics, intervention objectives, intervention content, intervention method, instructor characteristics and intervention fidelity, intervention outcomes, and research design.

3.2.1.1 Practitioner Characteristics

A total of 254 individuals (171 males and 83 females) from 21 studies participated in these interventions (Table 3.2). The chronological age (CA) of 230 practitioners was reported, and this ranged between 13 and 61 years (mean CA: 26.12 years). Of the 254 mindfulness practitioners, 178 were identified with ID. They were composed of 119 with mild ID, 21 with mild to moderate ID, seven with moderate ID, one with moderate/severe ID and 30 with an unspecified level of ID. The total number of practitioners included 47 with a range of comorbid psychiatric conditions including bipolar, schizophrenia and paedophilia, with the most common comorbid conditions being anxiety and psychotic disorder. The remaining 76 practitioners had ASD, of whom 73 were identified as without ID. In addition, 42 practitioners with ASD were reported to exhibit symptoms of depression, anxiety and rumination.

3.2.1.2 Intervention Objectives

Of the 21 interventions that made up category 1, 15 were concerned with the behavioural problems of individuals with DD. The most common behavioural objective was to control aggressive behaviour (e.g. Adkins, Singh, Winton, McKeegan, & Singh, 2010; Chilvers, Thomas, & Stanbury, 2011; Lew, Matta, Tripp-Tebo, & Watts, 2006; Singh, Wahler, Adkins, & Myers, 2003; Singh et al., 2007a, 2013a). Other objectives were ceasing smoking (Singh et al., 2011a, 2013b, 2014a), controlling deviant sexual arousal (Singh et al., 2011e) and losing weight (Singh et al., 2008a).

Within the 15 studies addressing the behavioural problems of individuals with DD, seven applied mindfulness practice to individuals with a dual diagnosis of ID accompanied by a psychiatric disorder (Adkins et al., 2010; Chilvers et al., 2011; Lew et al., 2006; Singh et al., 2003, 2007a, 2008b, 2011e). For this cohort, the most common reason to practise mindfulness was to control aggressive behaviours. For individuals with ID but without mental health issues, the main reasons to participate in mindfulness interventions were to cease smoking (Singh et al., 2011a, 2013b,

Table 3.2 Mindfulness interventions for individuals with DD

Intervention study	Intervention objective	Mindfulness practitioner	Intervention content	Intervention method	Instructor/Fidelity	Outcome measure	Intervention design
1. Singh et al. (2003)	Reduce aggression to maintain community placement	27-year-old male with dual disability (mild ID and psychotic disorder)	Meditation on soles of the feet (SoF)	Individual training (1) 30-minute role-play and practice twice a day for 5 days and (2) 1 week of homework practice assignments	Instructor not stated Fidelity not stated	(1) Incidents of aggression and restraints; (2) Self-control; (3) Staff and resident injuries; (4) Medication; and (5) Community activities	Single subject Baseline: 5 mths Intervention: 12 mths Follow-up: 12 mths
2. Singh et al. (2007a)	Reduce aggression to maintain community placement	Two male and one female adults (CA: 27, 43 and 39 yrs) with dual disability (moderate ID and mental illness)	Meditation on SoF	Individual training (1) Guided meditation (1 wk) and rehearsing several times per day Dot sticker on the practitioners' SoF & cue and (2) Audiotape of instructions for self- practice	First author Fidelity not stated	(1) Incidents of targeted aggressive behaviour	Multiple baseline design across participants Baseline: 3, 5 and 10 wks Intervention: 35 wks Follow-up: 2 yrs
3. Singh et al. (2008b)	Reduce aggression for transition to community placement	Six male offenders (CA: 25, 28, 34, 23, 25 and 36 yrs) with dual disability (ID and mental illness)	Meditation on SoF	Individual training (1) Guided meditation and (2) Practise twice a day	Therapist not stated fidelity not stated	(1) Incidents of (physical and verbal) aggression & restraints (2) Staff & resident injuries (3) Medication	Multiple baseline design across participants Baseline: About 3–8 wks Intervention: 27 mths

Table 3.2 (continued)

Intervention study	Intervention objective	Mindfulness practitioner	Intervention content	Intervention method	Instructor/Fidelity	Outcome measure	Intervention design
4. Adkins et al. (2010)	Reduce aggression to maintain community placement	Two male and one female adults (CA: 42, 25 & 22 yrs) with dual disability (mild ID & mental illness)	Meditation on SoF	Individual training (1) 1 h a day, 5 days a week (Use audio tape or parent-mediation) (2) Practise twice a day	Community-based therapist Fidelity not stated	Incidents of targeted maladaptive behaviours Subjective and psychological measures	Multiple baseline design across participants Baseline: 2–4 wks Intervention: 2–5 wks Self-practice: 12–26 wks Follow-up: 4–8 wks
5. Chilvers et al. (2011)	Reduce aggression	15 females (CA: 18–47) with mild to moderate ID in a forensic medium secure psychiatric ward	Mindfulness activities as part of DBT:Participation (fully engrossed in an activity) Observation (attend to the observation target) Description (providing a factual description)	Group exercise Individual feedback Awareness training to all nursing staff	Facilitators received supervision from a consultant clinical psychologist Fidelity not stated	*(1) Incidents of aggression* *(2) physical restraints* *(3) seclusions*	Pre-post no-control group design Intervention: 5 mths (30 min twice a week)

Table 3.2 (continued)

Intervention study	Intervention objective	Mindfulness practitioner	Intervention content	Intervention method	Instructor/Fidelity	Outcome measure	Intervention design
6. Lew et al. (2006)	Reduce risk behaviour	Eight females (CA: 25–61) with dual disability (seven mild and one moderate ID & psychiatric disorder)	Mindfulness activities as part of dialectical behaviour therapy (DBT): mindful breathing, and observe and describe common objects; Distress tolerance; Emotion regulation; and Interpersonal effectiveness	Simplified language Pictorial representation: Use video characters to explain abstract concepts (i.e. reasonable mind, emotion mind and wise mind) Collaboration with residential caregivers	DBT clinicians Fidelity not stated	Incidents of risk behaviour	Pre-post no-control group design Intervention: 18 mths (1) Individual weekly therapy (1 h); (2) Group skills training sessions (2 h) for 23 weeks (of these 6 sessions devoted to mindfulness)
7. Singh et al. (2011b)	Reduce aggression and anger	Three male adults (CA: 28, 28 and 32 yrs) with mild ID	Meditation on SoF	Intervention initiated on request of practitioners Discussion on antecedents of aggression and anger Step-by-step repeated instruction on SoF Social gatherings with the trainer	33-year-old male with dual disability (mild ID and psychotic disorder) who learned the meditation on SoF six years ago Fidelity ensured by following the SoF procedure	Incidents of aggression and anger	Multiple baseline design across participants Baseline: 8–21 wks Intervention: 52−39 wks Follow-up: for 2 years

Table 3.2 (continued)

Intervention study	Intervention objective	Mindfulness practitioner	Intervention content	Intervention method	Instructor/Fidelity	Outcome measure	Intervention design
8. Singh et al. (2013a)	Reduce physical and verbal aggression	34 individuals (27 males and 7 females) with borderline to mild ID (Mean CA 23.25 yrs, range 17–34)	Introduction to the anger management programme Attention on arousal states Breathing meditation Meditation on SoF	Verbal instruction and modelling	Parents and support staff Fidelity assessed using the standard checklist Fidelity 89%–100% (mean=96%) across the parents- and support staff individual dyads	Incidents of physical and verbal aggression	Waiting list control design Intervention: 12wks Follow-up: 12wks
9. Singh et al. (2011c)	Reduce physical aggression	Three male adolescents (CA: 14, 16 and 17 yrs) with ASD	Meditation on SoF	Verbal instructions Prompts Self-practice with iPod audio recording The first author taught mothers	First author taught mothers Mothers taught sons Fidelity not stated	Incidents of aggressive behaviour	Multiple baseline design across participants Baseline: 3–10 wks Intervention: 5 days (30 min) Practice: 23–29 wks Follow up: 3 years

Table 3.2 (continued)

Intervention study	Intervention objective	Mindfulness practitioner	Intervention content	Intervention method	Instructor/Fidelity	Outcome measure	Intervention design
10. Singh et al. (2011d)	Reduce physical aggression	Three male adolescents (CA: 15, 13 & 18 yrs) with AS	Meditation on SoF	Verbal instructions Modelling Prompts Self-practice with iPod audio recording	First author taught mothers Mothers taught sons Initial teaching sessions were recorded and reviewed Training fidelity (100 %)	Incidents of aggressive behaviour	Multiple baseline design across participants Baseline: 3–6 wks Intervention: 5 days (15 min) Practice: 17–24 wk Follow-up: 4 years
11. Singh et al. (2011e)	Control deviant sexual arousal	Three male sexual offenders (CA: 34, 23 and 25 yrs) with dual disability (mild ID and mental illness)	(1) Meditation on SoF and (2) Mindful observation of thoughts	(1) Induce sexual arousal (use stimulus pictures from magazines) and switch attention to SoF and (2) Individualisation of meditation instruction and self-practice homework	Two therapists (very experienced and newly established in meditation) Fidelity not evaluated	Self-reported levels of sexual arousal	Multiple baseline design across participants: (1) Baseline: 5–8 wks; (2) 4 individual meetings (0.5–1 h) for the intervention period; (3) Intervention (SoF): 13 wks; and (4) Intervention (observation of thoughts): 35–40 wk

Table 3.2 (continued)

Intervention study	Intervention objective	Mindfulness practitioner	Intervention content	Intervention method	Instructor/Fidelity	Outcome measure	Intervention design
12. Singh et al. (2011a)	Cease smoking	A 31-year-old male heavy smoker with mild ID	(1) Intention; (2) Mindful observation of thoughts; and (3) Meditation on SoF	(1) Self-affirmation regarding intention to quit smoking; (2) Role-play and discussion; and 3) Self-practice: Meditation on the SoF	Therapist with extensive experience in mindfulness meditation and service delivery to individuals with ID Fidelity ensured by following the SoF procedure	Number of smoked cigarettes per day	Single subject Pre-baseline: 10–15 min breathing meditation twice a day for 3 mths Baseline: 14 days Intervention: 82 days Maintenance: 12 mths Follow-up: 3 yrs
13. Singh et al. (2013b)	Cease smoking	Three male adults (CA: 27, 31 and 23 years) with mild ID	(1) Intention: Verbal self-affirmation of intention to quit smoking; (2) Mindful observation of thoughts; and (3) Meditation on SoF	(1) Discussion to control a desire to smoke every morning; (2) Individualised verbal instruction; and (3) Role-play	Therapist with extensive experience in mindfulness meditation and service delivery to individuals with ID Fidelity ensured by following the SoF manual (100 %)	Number of smoked cigarettes	Multiple baseline design across participants Criterion (# of cigarette) changes: (1) Pre-baseline: Concentration meditation for 10–15 min twice a day for 3 mths; (2) Baseline: 10 days; (3) Intervention: About 110 days; (4) Maintenance: 12 mths; and (5) Follow-up: 3 yrs

Table 3.2 (continued)

Intervention study	Intervention objective	Mindfulness practitioner	Intervention content	Intervention method	Instructor/Fidelity	Outcome measure	Intervention design
14. Singh et al. (2014a)	Cease smoking	51 adults (41 males and 10 females) with mild ID (CA: 32.56 yrs, *SD*=10.29)	1) Intention: Verbal self-affirmation of intention to quit smoking; (2) Mindful observation of thoughts; and (3) Meditation on SoF	1) Discussion to control a desire to smoke every morning; (2) Individualised verbal instruction; and (3) Role-play	Therapist with extensive experience in mindfulness meditation and service delivery to individuals with ID Fidelity ensured by conducting observations of randomly selected audiotapes of the instruction sessions (100 %)	Number of smoked cigarettes	Randomised controlled trial: (1) Pre-baseline: Concentration meditation for 10–15 min twice a day for 1 mth; (2) Baseline: 4 wks; (3) Intervention: 36 weeks; and (4) Follow-up: 1 yr
15. Singh et al. (2008a)	Lose weight	A 17-year-old male adolescent with Prader–Willi syndrome and mild ID	(1) Mindful eating; (2) Visualising and labelling hunger; and (3) Meditation on SoF	(1) Not stated; (2) Use of a cartoon character; and (3) Individual training for a week	Mother as a therapist with assistance of senior author Fidelity not stated	Mean weight	Single subject Baseline: 12 mths Intervention exercise only: 12 mths Intervention exercise and food awareness: 12 mths Intervention exercise, food awareness and mindfulness: 24 mths Follow-up: every 3 mths for 3 yrs

Table 3.2 (continued)

Intervention study	Intervention objective	Mindfulness practitioner	Intervention content	Intervention method	Instructor/Fidelity	Outcome measure	Intervention design
16. Brown and Hooper (2009)	Reduce anxiety and obsessive thoughts	A 18-year-old female adolescent with dual disability	Body and thought awareness Acceptance and Commitment Therapy (ACT) Mindfulness exercises on body Metaphors to understand and defuse thoughts Goal settings skills	Individual training Activity-based exercise using drawings and real objects Prompts	First author implied Fidelity not stated	Adapted version of Acceptance and Action Questionnaire-9 Parental reports	Single case study Intervention: 6 mths (17 sessions) Follow-up: 4 mths
17. Idusohan-Moizer, Sawicka, Dendle and Albany (2013)	Reduce depression and anxiety Improve mental wellbeing	15 (8 females and 7 males) adults (mean CA 30.75yrs, range 21–44) with dual disability	Combination of MBCT: mindfulness of the breath, basic yoga stretches, the raisin exercise and diary of pleasant and unpleasant events ACT: Metaphors and analogies Meditation on SoF	PowerPoint slides of pictures illustrating the key points Handouts with home assignment instruction Meditation CD Emphasis on repetition and mastery	Clinical psychologist with training in mindfulness-based therapies Assistant psychologist and two trainee clinical psychologists who attended mindfulness workshops Fidelity not stated	Hospital Anxiety and Depression Scale Compassion Scale	Pre-post no-control group design Intervention: 9–10 wks (Weekly 1.5 h session) Follow-up: 6 wks

Table 3.2 (continued)

Intervention study	Intervention objective	Mindfulness practitioner	Intervention content	Intervention method	Instructor/Fidelity	Outcome measure	Intervention design
18. Spek, van Ham and Nyklicek (2013)	Reduce depression, anxiety and rumination Increase in positive affect	42 adults (27 males & 14 females) with ASD without ID (mean CA: 42.25 yrs, *SD*=11.05)	Modified MBCT (omitting cognitive elements) Mindful eating Mindful breathing Mindful walking Mindful sitting Psycho-education on ruminative thoughts and the relationship with ASD Movement exercise Body scan	Group training (10–11 people) Individual consultations on choice of types of meditation and best time to practise Mp3 audio files	Psychologist & clinical psychologist who were trained in MBCT Fidelity not stated	Symptom Checklist-90-revised Rumination-Reflection Questionnaire Dutch Global Mood Scale	Randomised controlled trial Intervention: 9 weeks (weekly sessions for 2.5 h)
19. Miodrag, Lense and Dykens (2013)	Examine stress-related physiological symptoms in relation to mindfulness practice	13 males and 11 females (Mean CA 27.5 yrs, range 16–40 yrs) with Williams Syndrome (Mean IQ score 70.7, range 43–91)	Modified MBSR: Qigong movement Breathing meditation Body awareness and scan Sitting meditation Loving kindness Mindfulness in everyday life	Small group Hand-over-hand modelling for Qigong Straightforward language Visual aid Real-life example	Three instructors trained in mindfulness interventions and working experience in the ID field Fidelity consideration: using scripts and following standards exercises from MBSR	Salivary cortisol and alpha-amylase (sAA) Self-reported levels of anxiety	Pre-post no-control group design Intervention: 5 days for 20 min

Table 3.2 (continued)

Intervention study	Intervention objective	Mindfulness practitioner	Intervention content	Intervention method	Instructor/Fidelity	Outcome measure	Intervention design
20. Pahnke, Lundgren, Hursti and Hirvikoski (2013)	Examine feasibility of modified ACT-based skills training	28 students (21 males and 7 females) with ASD from 6 special schools without ID (Mean CA 16.5 yrs, range 13–21 yrs)	Acceptance of thoughts, feelings and body sensations Self as context Worksheets connecting values to more direct behaviour goals Identifying barriers to and enablers of carrying out goal-directed behaviour Illustration of avoidance trap Seeing thoughts as thoughts Applications of learned behaviour strategies and mindfulness techniques in stressful situations	Two 40-min small groups (4–6 participants) sessions per week Teacher-facilitated 6 to 12 min of daily mindfulness exercises in the classroom using a CD containing instructions	Classroom teacher-facilitated daily mindfulness exercises Graduate psychology student under the supervision for group sessions No fidelity measure	Stress Survey Schedule (teacher - and self-ratings) Strengths and Difficulties Questionnaires (teacher- and self-ratings) Beck Youth Inventories (Self-ratings)	Quasi-experimental pilot study Intervention: 6 wks Follow-up: 2 mths

Table 3.2 (continued)

Intervention study	Intervention objective	Mindfulness practitioner	Intervention content	Intervention method	Instructor/Fidelity	Outcome measure	Intervention design
21. Sakdalan, Shaw and Collier (2010)	Examine the effects of modified DBT Coping Skills training for people with ID	6 forensic clients (5 males and 1 female, Mean CA 26.18 yrs) with mild to moderate ID (Mean IQ 57.17)	DBT Coping skills training: (1) Mindfulness; (2) Distress tolerance; (3) Emotional regulation; and (4) Interpersonal effectiveness	Group skill training: Role playing, formal teaching, experiential exercises Review of individual homework Structuring environment to support treatment	Facilitators without further info Fidelity not stated	Short-term assessment of risk and treatability Vineland Adaptive Behaviour Scales Health of the Nation Outcome Scales for people with learning disabilities Incident reports	Pre-post no-control group design Intervention: 13 weeks (sessions for 1.5 h)

2014a) and to reduce aggression (Singh et al., 2011b, 2013a). Finally, two studies applied mindfulness to individuals with ASD solely to manage their aggressive behaviours (Singh et al., 2011c, d).

The remaining six intervention studies in category 1 used mindfulness practice to alleviate the psychological difficulties of individuals with DD. Of these, four concerned individuals with ID and two concerned individuals with ASD. The most commonly addressed psychological problems of individuals with DD were anxiety and depression (Brown & Hooper, 2009; Idusohan-Moizer et al., 2013; Spek et al., 2013). The remaining three studies addressed these psychological issues by appropriately modifying programmes such as ACT (Pahnke et al., 2013), DBT (Sakdalant et al., 2010) and MBSR (Miodraget et al., 2013) for individuals with DD.

This overview of the objectives of mindfulness intervention studies in the field of DD and the characteristics of the mindfulness practitioners shows a pattern similar to that revealed by the previous systematic review (i.e. Hwang & Kearney, 2013). Researchers focused more on individuals with ID than on those with ASD, and were concerned more with behavioural rather than psychological problems. This pattern is now changing, and increased attention is now being paid to individuals with ASD and the psychological problems of individuals with ID more generally.

Having reviewed the kinds of problems addressed by the 21 intervention studies that directly address the difficulties of individuals with DD by training them in mindfulness, the following section examines the content of these interventions, principally the role played by mindfulness training, along with the intervention method employed and the outcomes attained.

3.2.1.3 Intervention Content

The content of these interventions is classified according to whether it was developed specifically to address the behavioural or psychological problems of individuals with ID, or whether it emerged from the modification of the already-existing mindfulness-based interventions (MBIs). Of the 21 studies that directly applied mindfulness to individuals with DD, 13 used a procedure that was specifically developed for these individuals. This is meditation on soles of the feet (SoF), practised either as the only component of the intervention or together with other types of practice. The remaining eight studies applied the existing MBIs, either individually or in combination. These were Dialectical Behaviour Therapy (DBT), Acceptance and Commitment Therapy (ACT), Mindfulness-based Stress Reduction (MBSR) and mindfulness-based cognitive therapy (MBCT). Intervention content is further discussed according to intervention objectives and mindfulness practice elements (Table 3.3).

In the studies under review, the most frequently employed mindfulness practice used to reduce the behavioural problems of individuals with DD has been Meditation on SoF. Singh et al. (2003) developed Meditation on SoF based on the concept

Table 3.3 Mindfulness practice elements

	Awareness of breathing	Awareness of bodily sensations	Awareness of actions	Awareness of mental states	Shifting attention	Concentration
SoF (Adkins et al., 2010; Singh et al., 2003, 2007a, 2008b, 2011b, c, d, 2013a)	I	I		I	I	
SoF + observe bodily sensation of hunger + mindful eating (Singh et al., 2008a)	I	I	I	I	I	
SoF + observe thought and desire for smoking + concentration meditation (Singh et al., 2011a, 2013b, 2014b)	I	I		I	I	I
SoF + observe sexually aroused thoughts (Singh et al., 2011e)	I	I		I	I	
DBT: mindful breathing (Chilvers et al., 2011; Lew et al., 2006; Sakdalan et al., 2010)	I			I		
ACT: Observe bodily movements and awareness of thoughts (Brown & Hooper, 2009; Pahnke et al., 2013)		I		I		
MBCT (Spek et al., 2013)	I	I	I	I		
MBSR (Miodrag et al., 2013)	I	I	I	I		
MBCT + ACT + SoF (Idusohan-Moizer et al., 2013)	I	I	I	I	I	

of mindfulness as "a clear, calm mind that is focused on the present moment" that allows the practitioner "to be aware not only of external conditions but also of internal ones, especially physiological arousal states" (p. 160). Meditation on SoF begins with the practitioner establishing her posture by sitting or standing with feet placed firmly on the floor, thus grounding the body, and then paying attention to her breathing, thus grounding the mind. The next stage involves reminding herself of the specifics of her arousal state, such as angry thoughts and feelings, and so stimulating the physical and mental symptoms of this state. The practitioner then directs attention to the soles of the feet until body and mind calm down. Mindfulness on SoF therefore contains awareness of breathing, bodily sensations (soles of the feet) and mental states (e.g. anger), and it also involves the technique of deliberately shifting attention from a disturbing mental state such as anger to a neutral object such as soles of the feet.

Meditation on SoF was taught along with observation of thoughts to control the deviant sexual arousal of three male adults with dual disability (Singh et al., 2011e). When applied to cease smoking (Singh et al., 2011a, 2013b, 2014a), Meditation on SoF was supported by concentration meditation. Practitioners with ID who were heavy smokers conducted regular concentration practice prior to learning Meditation on SoF. Concentration meditation involves maintaining a sustained attention on objects of awareness to induce calmness of mind, and traditionally it is often practised alongside mindfulness meditation (Bodhi, 1994; Pandita, 1993). Although in these studies the role of concentration meditation was not clearly stated, it appeared to be to assist practitioners to sustain their attention on SoF rather than to be consumed by thoughts and desires related to smoking.

Of the studies that drew their mindfulness practice techniques from the existing MBIs, those that employed DBT (e.g. Chilvers et al., 2011; Lew et al., 2006) focused on awareness of breathing and mental states (e.g. emotions) to reduce the behavioural problems of individuals with DD, while those that employed ACT (Brown & Hooper, 2009) emphasised awareness of bodily movements and mental states (e.g. thoughts) to meet the same intervention objective. Interventions that adopted MBCT or MBSR aimed to reduce the psychological problems or stress-related physiological symptoms in individuals with DD through enhancing awareness of breathing, bodily sensations and movements, and mental states (e.g. Miodrag et al., 2013; Spek et al., 2013).

3.2.1.4 Intervention Method

This section outlines intervention design, strategy and duration. Intervention design can be classified according to whether the mindfulness training and self-practice components were engaged in consecutively or concurrently. Of the 21 studies, 13 took the consecutive design approach, which consisted of an intensive training period followed by a self-practice period. During the intensive training period, practitioners individually learned Meditation on SoF though guided meditation and practice assignments. The clarity of instruction was enhanced by audio-recorded verbal instructions, role-play and modelling. These practitioners learned Meditation on SoF either as a sole component (e.g. Singh et al., 2003, 2007a) or along with mindful observation of thoughts (e.g. Singh et al., 2011a, e). Each training session lasted between 15 min and one hour. Practitioners then entered a self-practice period that ranged between 82 days and 27 months.

The remaining eight studies adopted the concurrent design approach, where mindfulness training took place alongside practice periods ranging from five days to 18 months. These studies drew on mindfulness practices from the existing MBI programmes, adjusted to meet the specific learning characteristics and requirements of individuals with DD. Adjustments took place in language, material, learning process and content (Table 3.4), most frequently in language and learning process. To meet the learning requirements of individuals with DD, language was simplified and abstract expressions were removed. Personalised care was provided through either individual consultation or small group training. Pictures and drawings were used to concretise abstract concepts such as mindfulness. The number of learning activities was limited to reduce the intellectual demands of the training.

The intervention periods for the 21 studies varied depending on intervention content, and ran between five days and 24 months. Studies that adopted Meditation on SoF tended to have a longer intervention period than those that employed modified MBI programmes. Of the 21 studies, 12 had a mindfulness intervention that extended for longer than 6 months. Of these, 10 taught mindfulness through Meditation on SoF. Intervention periods were also linked to the severity of participant's disabilities. Mindfulness practitioners with dual disability (e.g. Singh et al., 2003) or moderate to severe ID (e.g. Brown & Hooper, 2009) tended to participate in intervention studies for longer than 6 months, while those with mild ID (e.g. Singh et al., 2013a, b) or ASD without ID (e.g. Pahnke et al., 2013; Spek et al., 2013) participated for less than 6 months.

3.2.1.5 Instructor Characteristics and Intervention Fidelity

Instructor quality is critical for the outcomes of mindfulness interventions (Kabat-Zinn, 2003; Segal, Williams, & Teasdale, 2002). Mindfulness instructors require not just an intellectual understanding of mindfulness but also an experiential understanding, gained through prolonged mindfulness practice (Grossman, 2010). Mindfulness instructors for individuals with DD also require knowledge of individuals with DD (Hwang & Kearney, 2013), who often have learning requirements that call for a wide range of supports (Kaiser & McIntyre, 2010).

Some 20 of the 21 studies stated that they used mindfulness instructors, and of these six (Miodrag et al., 2013; Singh et al., 2011a, b, e, 2013b, 2014a) employed instructors whose knowledge and experience of both mindfulness and individuals with DD were clearly explained. As shown in Table 3.2, nine studies did not pro-

Table 3.4 Adjustment areas of the existing mindfulness-based psychotherapy programmes

Adjustment area	Language	Material	Learning process	Content
DBT (Chilvers et al., 2011)	Brief and simplified expressions	–	–	–
DBT (Lew et al., 2006)	Simplified terms and ideas	Pictorial representation	Small group training Individualised care	–
DBT (Sakdalan et al., 2010)	–	Pictures, drawings and real objects	–	–
ACT (Brown & Hooper, 2009)	–	Pictures, drawings and real objects	Provision of additional sessions Provision of time to process information Activity-based learning	–
ACT (Pahnke et al., 2013)	–	–	Small group	Shorter exercises Reduced number of visualising metaphors Additional mindfulness exercises focusing on sensory issues
MBCT (Spek et al., 2013)	Removal of abstract expressions	–	Individualised care	–
ACT + MBCT + Meditation on SoF (Idusohan-Moizer et al., 2013)	Simple language	Pictorial presentation Concrete examples	Repetition and mastery Provision of time to process information	Reduced number of home activities
MBSR (Miodrag et al., 2013)	Removal of abstract expressions and jargon	–	Repetition Provision of time to process information	–

vide information regarding the instructors' background in mindfulness or individuals with DD, but confined themselves to general comments such as whether the instructors were therapists, facilitators or psychologists.

Family and professional care providers gain an understanding of individuals with DD from their lived experience over time. This understanding was utilised by five studies that employed parents and professional staff as mindfulness instructors. For example, family care providers of individuals with ASD (Singh et al., 2011c, 2011d), and family and professional care providers of individuals with ID (Singh et al., 2008a, 2013a), delivered mindfulness activities to their care recipients. Prior to the intervention, an experienced mindfulness teacher trained these novice teachers in the procedural steps of Meditation on SoF.

Intervention fidelity is a critical methodological feature of any sound intervention study. It requires a demonstration that an intervention is delivered as planned (Dumas, Lynch, Laughlin, Phillips Smith, & Prinz, 2001). Of the 21 studies, only seven reported intervention fidelity. Of the seven, four studies ensured intervention fidelity by following scripts or procedural instructions regarding mindfulness activities (Singh et al., 2011b, d, 2013b). The other three studies evaluated intervention fidelity by using a checklist provided by a manual (Singh et al., 2013a) and reviewing recordings of intervention sessions (Singh et al., 2011d, 2014a).

3.2.1.6 Intervention Outcomes

All studies reported positive outcomes of mindfulness interventions for individuals with DD. A total of 10 studies that aimed to address the aggression of individuals with DD through mindfulness reported major decreases (e.g. zero or near-zero incidents) in physical and/or verbal aggression at the conclusion of the interventions (Adkins et al., 2010; Chilvers et al., 2011; Lew et al., 2006; Singh et al., 2003, 2007a, 2008b, 2011b, c, d, 2013a). In three studies where cessation of smoking was targeted, the number of smoked cigarettes was reduced to zero (Singh et al., 2011a, 2013b) or to a level of statistical significance (Singh et al., 2014a). A practitioner with Prader–Willi syndrome demonstrated weight loss from 249.8 lb to 200 lb (Singh et al., 2008a), and three practitioners with dual disability showed reductions of deviant sexual arousal from the maximum level of 12 to 2.95, 3.03 and 1.51 respectively (Singh et al., 2011e).

The six remaining intervention studies drew mindfulness practices from the existing mindfulness-based psychotherapy programmes to alleviate anxiety and depression of individuals with DD. Participants in modified MBCT programmes with ASD (Spek et al., 2013) and dual disability (Idusohan-Moizer et al., 2013) showed statistically significant reductions in anxiety and depression. The parents of a young female adult with dual disability, who struggled with anxiety and depression, reported that their daughter appeared to have a calmer mind and experienced shorter rumination periods following a modified ACT programme (Brown & Hooper, 2009). A school-based modified ACT programme involving 28 young adults with

ASD resulted in reductions in stress, including emotional stress, and hyperactivity (Pahnke et al., 2013), while a five-day modified MBSR programme for 24 adults with Williams Syndrome resulted in reductions in stress-related physiological symptoms (Miodrag et al., 2013). A modified DBT programme for six adults with ID that ran for 13 weeks showed a decrease in the level of risk based on the short-term assessment of risk and treatability (START) along with an increase in global functioning (Sakdalan et al., 2010).

In conclusion, all intervention studies based on modifications to the existing mindfulness-based psychotherapy programmes reported positive intervention outcomes for practitioners with DD. However, it is difficult to distinguish how much of these positive outcomes can be accounted for by mindfulness practice as distinct from the other elements that characterised the intervention, such as carrying out goal-directed behaviour and the interpersonal relationships developed in the course of the intervention.

3.2.1.7 Research Design

Research design has diversified since the period covered by the first review, when 10 out of 12 studies adopted single-subject design as a way of examining the effects of mindfulness intervention for individuals with DD (Hwang & Kearney, 2013). For the 21 category-1 studies included in the current review, single-subject design remains the most frequently employed research design, with 12 studies using it in eight multiple-subject and four single-subject studies. A major difference in the current review is the use of experimental design, which was employed in four studies. A randomised control trial was employed in two studies (i.e. Singh et al., 2014a; Spek et al., 2013), which provided more weight to their results. Of the remaining two studies, one adopted a waiting list control (Singh et al., 2013a) and the other a quasi-experimental design (Pahnke et al., 2013). The number of studies adopting a pre-post, no-control group design also increased from two in the previous review to five in the current review (Chilvers et al., 2011; Idusohan-Moizer et al., 2013; Lew et al., 2006; Miodrag et al., 2013; Sakdalan et al., 2010).

This section provides a summary of the category 1 interventions, which support individuals with DD directly by training them in mindfulness. More studies addressed the behavioural problems of individuals with DD than their psychological problems, and the intervention needs of individuals with ID rather than those with ASD. This pattern is similar to that found in the first systematic review (Hwang & Kearney, 2013). The pattern is changing with the diversification of intervention objectives and content, as a growing number of studies have focused on reducing the psychological problems of individuals with DD by training them in mindfulness practices drawn from the existing MBIs.

Mindfulness was often used as the central component of interventions when addressing behavioural problems and as part of an existing psychotherapy programme when addressing psychological problems. These studies together demonstrated that individuals with DD could reduce their behavioural and psychological problems through practising mindfulness. The next sections focus on intervention studies that support individuals with DD indirectly, by training their family or professional care providers in mindfulness.

3.2.2 *Mindful Care: Training Family or Professional Care Providers in Mindfulness*

Category 1 mindfulness interventions were those that applied mindfulness directly to individuals with DD, by training them in mindfulness. Category 2 interventions apply mindfulness indirectly, by training the family or professional care providers of individuals with DD in mindfulness. We were interested in knowing how mindfulness training would affect the quality of care these individuals were provided with and therefore their quality of life. A total of eight category-2 intervention studies were identified, of which five trained family care providers and three trained professional care providers. As with the category 1 interventions, some studies—specifically those conducted by Singh's research team—employed an independent approach to mindfulness training, while others adapted their approach to mindfulness from established MBIs, in this case MBSR and MBCT.

3.2.2.1 Practitioner Characteristics and Intervention Objectives

The most frequently targeted objective in these interventions was the behavioural problems of individuals with DD, and in particular the reduction of aggressive behaviours. Of the eight studies, seven (Bögels, Hellemans, Deursen, Römer, & Meulen, 2013; Neece, 2013; Singh et al., 2006a, b, 2007b, 2009, 2014b) were aimed at the behavioural problems of care recipients while one (Singh et al., 2004) targeted their psychological problems. Regarding participants, one study (Singh et al., 2007) included individuals with DD and three (Singh et al., 2004, 2006a, 2009) individuals with a specified ID. Two interventions (Singh et al., 2006b, 2014b) focused on individuals with ASD. The final two studies included individuals with ASD as one aspect of developmental delays (Bögels et al., 2013; Neece, 2013).

3.2.2.2 Intervention Content, Method and Outcomes

Family Care Providers

Beginning with the five studies that provided mindfulness training to the family members of individuals with DD, Singh et al. (2006b) individually trained three mothers of young children with ASD and aggressive behaviour in mindfulness in 12 two-hour sessions that took place three times a week, each third week. The form of mindfulness training used was not taken from any existing MBI, although the topics in the training modules show similarities to those of the MBSR training programme. Mindfulness was defined as "having a clear, calm mind that is focused on the present moment" (Singh et al., 2006b, p. 170). The modules featured topics drawn from a variety of sources, such as Zen and insight meditation. These included Knowing Mind and Attention, Beginner's Mind, Being Your Child, Nonjudgmental Acceptance, Loving-kindness and Using Mindfulness in Daily Interactions. Mothers continued to practise formal and daily mindfulness activities over 52 weeks and maintained a record of their child's problem behaviour. The outcomes were positive. Over the training and practice periods, the three children demonstrated gradual but significant same as that of the parent mindfulness training studies reductions in aggressive behaviours, noncompliance and self-injury. Mothers also benefited directly from their mindfulness training, through increased levels of satisfaction in their interactions with their children and with their parenting.

Singh et al. (2007b) delivered another mindfulness training programme to four mothers of children with DD and aggressive behaviours, using the same intervention content and design as Singh et al. (2006b). The children displayed a significant reduction in aggressive behaviours and an incremental increase in social interactions, as observed in a playroom at a day-care centre. In this study, the authors observed not only increased mother–child interaction satisfaction and parenting satisfaction, but also statistically significant decreases in parental stress ($t(3)=7.72$, $p<.01$), measured with the Parenting Stress Index at pre- and post-training. The authors suggested that parent mindfulness training is at least as effective as other forms of parent training in addressing children's maladaptive behaviour.

The most recent study (Singh et al., 2014b) examines the effects of Mindfulness-based Positive Behaviour Support (MBPBS), a newly developed 8-week mindfulness programme paired with the concept and techniques of Positive Behaviour Support (PBS). The MBPBS programme included a variety of meditation theories and practices taken from a variety of sources, including insight meditation, Zen and Tibetan Buddhism. It was provided to three mothers (CA 43, 37, 41 years) of young adults with ASD and challenging behaviours (CA 15, 16, 19 years) who were already familiar with PBS techniques. Mothers implemented PBS within the context of the mindfulness practices during the intervention period (i.e., 8 weeks) and self-practice period (i.e., 30–37 weeks). The outcomes were positive. Children who received care from their MBPBS-trained mothers demonstrated decreases in challenging behaviours and increases in pro-social behaviours (i.e. compliance with their mother's requests) during the practice period and further improvements in the same areas at the conclusion of the practice period. Mothers also benefited from this intervention, with statistically significant decreases in their perceived stress.

Due to the small sample size of these three studies caution must be taken in interpreting their results; however, the results of a recently conducted randomly controlled trial provide further evidence of the link between parental mindfulness and the behavioural problems of their children. Neece (2013) provided a standard MBSR training to 46 parents (Mean CA: 35 years) of young children (Mean CA: 3.8 years) with DD. The difference between pre- and post-test results indicates significant reductions in self-reported parenting stress and depression, along with increases in satisfaction with life. Interestingly, among the children of these parents the author also found significant reductions in ADHD symptoms and marginally significant reductions in attention problems. Based on these results, Neece concluded that reduced parenting stress was associated with reduced child behavioural problems.

Bögels et al. (2013) applied mindfulness to parenting attitudes, styles and stress in the mindful parenting programme, which combined elements from MBSR and MBCT. Some 86 parents (aged between 28 and 64, nine of whom were fathers) attended weekly training sessions over eight weeks. Their children had been clinically referred to mental health services. Nearly half were diagnosed with ADHD, while 15 % were diagnosed with ASD and 7 % with an anxiety disorder. Parents practised awareness of each moment and learned how to recognise the patterns and symptoms of their stress, and to become less reactive in their parenting.

The results for children included small-to-medium effect size improvements in internalising (e.g. anxiety and depression) and externalising (e.g. aggression) symptoms at post-intervention and follow-up (Bögels et al., 2013). Parents showed improvement in some domains of parenting skills (i.e. autonomy encouragement and overprotection) and co-parenting skills (i.e. reductions in conflicts in front of their child). Although parenting stress was one focus of the Mindful Parenting programme, the level of parenting stress was not measured.

Professional Care Providers

In a study aimed at professional care providers, Singh et al. (2009) provided mindfulness training to 23 group home staff members responsible for 20 individuals with ID in four group homes. Staff attended 12 two-hour weekly training sessions over 3 months and practised mindfulness at work for 6 months. The mindfulness training content was the same as that of the parent mindfulness training studies (e.g. Singh et al., 2006b, 2007b) except for changes that reflected the context of the staff–client relationship rather than that of the parent–child relationship. Their clients showed decreases in aggressive behaviours, verbal redirections made by staff to avoid aggression, the use of physical restraints and Stat medicine for uncontrolled aggression, and staff and peer injuries (Singh et al., 2009).

Two studies compared the effects of training professional care providers in mindfulness on the one hand and behavioural interventions on the other. In a study of six professional care providers of three individuals with profound ID, Singh et al. (2004) gave three of them mindfulness training and three behavioural training. These individuals with ID showed more signs of physical happiness (e.g. smiles) during their interactions with their care providers trained in mindfulness than during their interactions with caregivers trained in behavioural interventions. In another study, Singh et al. (2006a) gave behavioural training to 15 care providers of 18 individuals with ID and followed this up with mindfulness training after a 30- to 53-week gap. They noticed greater reductions in the aggressive behaviours of these care recipients with ID after their care providers' mindfulness training than after their behavioural training. While it is possible that the results of the mindfulness training were influenced by those of the earlier behavioural training, this study nevertheless suggests that mindfulness training for carers can enhance outcomes for individuals with ID.

Looking at the outcomes, the most frequently reported indirect effects of mindfulness training for family care providers were reductions in the aggressive behaviours of their care recipients. These results were accompanied by increased mother–child interaction satisfaction and parenting satisfaction. A similar pattern was identified in intervention studies concerning professional care providers, which reported increased quality of interactions (e.g. verbal instructions rather than physical restraints, more physical signs of happiness) and raised satisfaction with care services. These patterns suggest the existence of transactional relationships between the behavioural and psychological problems of care recipients on the one hand and care provider–care recipient interaction on the other. The key variable appears to be the quality of interaction, and this can be improved by mindfulness practice for care providers.

Having surveyed category 1 and category 2 interventions, those that apply mindfulness respectively to individuals with DD themselves or to their care providers, we will now move to category 3 interventions. These interventions are characterised by the provision of mindfulness training to both individuals with DD and to their care providers.

3.2.3 Mindful Learning and Mindful Care: Mindfulness Interventions to Those with DD and Their Care Providers

This is the smallest category in the review. Only two intervention studies have trained both children with DD and their parents in mindfulness and examined its effects on both parties. Bögels, Hoogstad, van Dun, de Schutter and Restifo (2008) provided eight weekly MBCT sessions to a group of parents and their 14 adolescent children. Some 79% of these parents had disorders such as depressive disorder, post-traumatic stress disorder or ASD, while their children were diagnosed with ADHD (2), ODD/CD (8) or ASD (4). The children practiced a modified form of MBCT appropriate to their age. Both parents and children reported substantial improvements in attaining their personal goals. The children also reported improvements in attention, mindful awareness and happiness. These results were maintained at an 8-week follow-up.

The final study (Russell, 2011) is a personal story written by the father of twin boys with Asperger's syndrome whose mindfulness practice was self-taught. He did not record the details of his training, and we know only that he was committed to a daily practice. This practice resulted in enhanced sensitivity to his thinking along with some control over it. He felt happier and had greater enjoyment with his twins. He devised and delivered his own mindfulness intervention for his twins, involving mindfulness of breathing. He reported that it was still too early at the time of writing to evaluate the effects of mindfulness on his children's thinking, although they appeared to handle anxiety better. As a parent of children with ASD, Russell (2011) commented on the paucity of information available for teaching mindfulness to individuals with ASD and called for more information and research.

3.2.4 Mindfulness Interventions Across and Beyond Categories

As noted earlier, the greatest concerns for families and professional workers in the field of DD arise from the behavioural problems of individuals with DD (Hastings, 2002; James, 2013). It is therefore understandable that reduction of behavioural problems is the most frequently targeted objective in the mindfulness intervention studies reviewed here. This pattern is consistent across category 1 studies (teaching mindfulness to individuals with DD) and category 2 studies (teaching mindfulness to family or professional care providers). In addition, more interventions were aimed at individuals living with ID than those with ASD, again across the two categories. For example, in the 21 category-1 studies there are only four that teach mindfulness to individuals with ASD.

While MBIs are not specifically designed to target the aggressive behaviours of individuals with DD per se, taken together the category 2 mindfulness intervention studies tell us that training the caregivers of individuals with DD in mindfulness can help to alleviate behavioural problems in individuals with DD. The mindfulness, empathy and loving-kindness cultivated by caregivers may contribute to the creation of a therapeutic milieu within which the behaviour of individuals with DD are accepted rather than controlled (Singh et al., 2006a). In addition, when parents and caregivers practise mindfulness they may become more sensitive to the habitual interactions that normally occur with little or no clear awareness and that often play a critical role in dysfunctional relationships (Dumas, 2005). These indirect or transactional effects suggest an additional avenue to reach out to individuals with DD, especially those with very complex educational needs, who might not be ready to practise mindfulness for themselves. The unique nature of mindfulness interventions is further discussed in the following sections.

3.3 Mindfulness, an Alternative Intervention Approach

In this section we briefly review other intervention approaches used for individuals with DD in response to their behavioural and psychological problems. Wherever possible, the strengths and limitations of these approaches will be compared with those of MBIs in order to identify the unique nature of mindfulness practice and discover areas where future mindfulness intervention studies could improve on current research.

There have been a number of approaches that have been used to manage the problem behaviours of individuals with DD. Pharmacotherapy provides one such approach, but it has been seen to have serious limitations (Williamson & Martin, 2012). There are concerns about the adverse effects on the health and quality of life of people with DD who undergo such interventions (Raghavan & Patel, 2010), along with the unanticipated physiological and psychological reactions associated with it (Otis & King, 2008). Consequently, a consensus has emerged that psychotropic medication should not be the first treatment option (Benson & Brooks, 2008).

Another approach to managing challenging behaviours has been through behavioural intervention, often in the domain of Applied Behaviour Analysis (ABA) (Matson, Mahan, & Matson, 2009). ABA is a systematic approach that assesses and modifies a targeted behaviour using precise and repeated measurement based on two basic assumptions: behaviours that are followed by reinforcers will occur more frequently in the future; and those that are followed by punishment will occur less frequently (Jackson & Panyan, 2002). Challenging behaviours are viewed as having been learned and therefore as capable of being unlearned. Family or professional care providers learn to assess what the function of a target behaviour is for an individual with DD, and then create a plan to develop a set of skills that can meet that function more skilfully (Heflin & Alaimo, 2006).

Although this approach is systematic and empirical, and has been used successfully in the management of aggressive behaviours of learners with DD (e.g. Lucyshyn, Albin, Horner, Mann, & Wadsworth, 2007), it has some limitations. Over-reliance on extrinsic rewards tends to overlook the intrinsic motivations of learners, while dependence on the adults delivering behavioural consequences can create a power imbalance (Kohn, 1993). In addition, it has been suggested that over-reliance on external agents, such as family and professional care providers, can limit the degree to which learned behaviours generalise into other settings (Jackson & Panyan, 2002). Finally, a narrow focus on discrete target behaviours can create an environment where these behaviours are viewed instrumentally, as merely something to be controlled.

MBIs appear to address these limitations of pharmacological and behavioural interventions. For example, when individuals with DD practise Meditation on SoF—to date the most frequently used mindfulness procedure for this population—they develop the capacity to notice their own psychological or physiological symptoms of anger. They then learn to relax their body and mind by shifting attention to their breathing and the sensations on the soles of their feet. Although teaching this practice requires external supports such as teachers and guided meditations, the practice of mindfulness occurs within the practitioners with DD themselves. Extrinsic rewards do not appear to play a crucial role. As individuals with DD develop skill in mindfulness, they become sensitive to the changes in their own minds and bodies and therefore become more skilled in managing their own behaviour. This has the additional benefit of making them more independent.

The practice of mindfulness has the potential to empower people with DD to address their problems by themselves, but only if they are motivated enough to make a strong and ongoing commitment to their practice. This raises the question of the difficulty for them to find the appropriate motivation. This issue, however, has not been fully addressed in the existing literature. Only two studies in this review (i.e. Bögels et al., 2008; Brown & Hooper, 2009) spoke of the extensive levels of support that are required for learners with DD to stay on task.

Mindfulness practice is also playing a useful role in addressing the psychological problems of individuals with DD. Cognitive behaviour therapy (CBT), which lacks a mindfulness component, has traditionally been used to address the psychological problems of individuals living with DD (Matson et al., 2009), such as stress, anxiety and mood swings. However, the identification of unhelpful thoughts and behaviours requires a verbal exchange between therapist and client, and this can be challenging for individuals with ID (Idusohan-Moizer et al., 2013). The more recent mindfulness-based psychotherapy programmes such as MBCT, ACT and DBT, considered the third wave of CBT therapies, have demonstrated greater potential for this population because they focus less on verbal appraisal and exchange and more on training the capacity of individuals with DD to be aware of their own physical sensations and mental events, thus developing the potential to be able to let them go (Idusohan-Moizer et al., 2013). However, modifying the existing MBIs may not be enough to address the unique learning characteristics and requirements of individuals with DD. In other words, a need exists for the development of mindfulness intervention programmes that specifically address the psychological issues of individuals with DD.

3.4 Conclusion

Some clear conclusions have emerged from our systematic review of 31 mindfulness-based interventions for individuals living with DD. To date, mindfulness-based interventions have focused more on the behavioural problems of individuals with DD than on their psychological problems. This reflects the fact that the challenging behaviour of people with DD is the major cause of burnout in family members and professional staff (Hastings & Browns, 2002; James, 2013). It is more common for these interventions to address these problems directly, by training individuals with DD, rather than indirectly, by training the family and professional caregivers of individuals with DD. Also, individuals with ID have received more attention than those with ASD in learning mindfulness to address their life issues. Recent studies have extended the scope of MBIs by looking at the psychological and physiological effects of mindfulness practice in individuals with DD. Another feature of recent studies is the use of a randomised control trial, which diversifies research design and provides more weight to their results.

This review has revealed several areas requiring further investigation. One important issue concerns the indirect or transactional effects of mindfulness training. While eight studies (e.g. Singh et al., 2006a) reported on the indirect effects of mindfulness practice, their nature and developmental trajectories are yet to be fully explored. More attention needs to be given to how the mindfulness practice of family and professional caregivers influences their care recipients. In addition, while several studies (e.g. Russel, 2011) involved family or professional caregivers teaching mindfulness to their care recipients with DD, there was no examination of the experience of these care providers as they fulfilled their roles of mindfulness teachers.

This brings us to the important issue of the role of a mindfulness teacher. It can be argued that to be appropriately qualified to teach mindfulness practice, a person requires theoretical knowledge and practical experience regarding both mindfulness and the population they teach (Hwang & Kearney, 2013). Training caregivers who already have substantial knowledge of individuals with DD could, therefore, be advantageous, provided they themselves are provided with sufficient theoretical and practical training in mindfulness and its practice. The existing intervention studies have taught mindfulness to trainers only to the extent that they could reproduce the procedures found in a manual, when they themselves have not undergone an extensive training in mindfulness. Educating trainers in the theoretical and practical aspects of mindfulness practice may be necessary for mindfulness to reach its potential to directly and indirectly affect the lives of individuals with DD.

Another issue that requires attention, given the limited number of relevant intervention studies, is how mindfulness is to be taught to individuals with ASD and/or ID (Chapman & Mitchell, 2013). While programmes such as MBSR provide a standardised approach to teaching mindfulness, programmes designed to teach individuals with ASD must match the degree of individuality in their condition (Shapiro, 2009). This is reflected in the ways in which MBIs that have been applied to individuals with DD have been modified to meet their learning requirements, with the aim of making the content straightforward and concrete, and the delivery clear and brief. The development of Meditation on SoF for individuals with DD and their care providers demonstrates the potential for creating new forms of mindfulness practice for the specific needs and characteristics of this population.

Finally, the forms of mindfulness training that have been applied to people with DD, including both modified MBIs such as MBSR, MBCT, ACT and DBT, as well as Meditation on SoF, have all been based on the particular understanding of mindfulness that has emerged from the lineage that runs from the modern Burmese movement through the work of Nyanaponika Thera and the various streams of contemporary North American Buddhism that have been influenced by it. It remains to be seen how alternative understandings of mindfulness-based training adapted, for example, directly from early Buddhist texts such as the Nikāyas, might be useful in rethinking both the nature of mindfulness itself and how it may be adapted to the varied characteristics and requirements of people with DD. The following chapter describes our recent study that explored these issues by training mothers of children with ASD and challenging behaviours to become mindfulness teachers for their own children.

This chapter began with the questions of what happens to individuals with DD when they practise mindfulness and what happens to individuals with DD when their family and professional care providers practise mindfulness? The answers that have emerged are, in brief, that individuals with DD learned to better manage their own behavioural or psychological problems, and they enjoyed the benefits of improved care from their care providers who had been trained in mindfulness.

References

ABS. (2012). Australian social trends (Vol. 2014). Canberra: Australian Bureau of Statistics.

Adkins, A. D., Singh, A. N., Winton, A. S. W., McKeegan, G. F., & Singh, J. (2010). Using a mindfulness-based procedure in the community: Translating research to practice. *Journal of Child Family Studies, 19,* 175–183.

American Psychiatric Association. (2013). *Diagnostic and statistical manual of mental disorders* (5th ed.). Arlington: American Psychiatric Publishing.

Benson, B. A., & Brooks, W. T. (2008). Aggressive challenging behaviour and intellectual disability. *Current Opinion in Psychiatry, 21,* 454–458.

Bodhi, B. (1994). *The noble eightfold path: Way to the end of suffering* (2nd ed.). Kandy: Buddhist Publication Society.

Bögels, S., Hoogstad, B., van Dun, L., de Schutter, S., & Restifo, K. (2008). Mindfulness training for adolescents with externalising disorders and their parents. *Behavioural and Cognitive Psychotherapy, 36,* 193–209.

Bögels, S., Hellemans, J., Deursen, S. v., Römer, M., & Meulen, R. v. d. (2013). Mindful parenting in mental health care: Effects on parental and chil 1997–2008. Pediatrics, d psychology, parental stress, parenting, coparenting, and marital functioning. *Mindfulness*. doi:10.1007/s12671-013-0209-7.

Boyle, G. A., Boulet, S., Schieve, L. A., Cohen, R. A., Blumberg, S. J., Yeargin-Allsopp, M., Visser, S., & Kogan, M. D. (2011). Trends in the Prevalence of Developmental Disabilities in US Children, 1997–2008. *Pediatrics*, *127*(6), 1034–1042. doi:10.1542/peds.2010-2989.

Brown, F. J., & Hooper, S. (2009). Acceptance and Commitment Theraphy (ACT) with a learning disabled young person experiencing anxious and obsessive thoughts. *Journal of Intellectual Disabilities, 13,* 195–201.

CDC. (2012). Prevalence of Autism Spectrum disorders-autism and developmental disabilities monitoring network, 14 Sites, United States, 2008. Atlanta: Centers for Disease Control and Prevention.

Centers for Disease Control and Prevention. (2013). Developmental Disabilities. http://www.cdc.gov/ncbddd/developmentaldisabilities/index.html. Zugegriffen: 2. Feb. 2014.

Chapman, M., & Mitchell, D. (2013). Mindfully valuing people now: An evaluation of introduction to mindfulness workshops for people with intellectual disabilities. *Mindfulness, 4,* 168–178.

Chilvers, J., Thomas, C., & Stanbury, A. (2011). The impact of a ward-based mindfulness programme on recorded aggression in a medium secure facility for women with learning disabilities. *Journal of Learning Disabilities and Offending Behaviour, 2,* 27–41.

de Ruiter, K. P., Dekker, M. C., Verhulst, F. C., & Koot, H. M. (2007). Developmental course of psychopathology in youth with and without intellectual disabilities. *Journal of Child Psychology and Psychiatry, 48*(5), 498–507.

Dumas, J. (2005). Mindfulness-based parent training: Strategies to lessen the grip of automaticity in families with disruptive children. *Journal of Clinical Child & Adolescent Psychology, 34,* 779–791.

Dumas, J., Lynch, A., Laughlin, J., Phillips Smith, E., & Prinz, R. (2001). Promoting intervention fidelity. Conceptual issues, methods and preliminary results from the early alliance prevention trial. *American Journal of Preventitive Medicine, 20,* 38–47.

Emerson, E. (2003). Prevalence of psychiatric disorders in children and adolescents with and without intellectual disability. *Journal of Intellectual Disability Research, 47,* 51–58.

Greya, I., Pollardb, J., McCleanc, B., MacAuleyd, N., & Hastings, R. (2010). Prevalence of psychiatric diagnoses and challenging behaviors in a community-based population of adults with intellectual disability. *Journal of Mental Health Research in Intellectual Disabilities, 3,* 210–222.

Grossman, P. (2010). Mindfulness for psychologists: Paying kind attention to the perceptible. *Mindfulness, 1,* 87–97.

Hastings, R. (2002). Do challenging behaviours affect staff psychological well-being? Issues of causality and mechanism. *American Journal on Mental Retardation, 107,* 455–467.

Hastings, R. (2005). Staff in special education settings and behaviour problems: Towards a framework for research and practice. *Educational Psychology, 25,* 207–221.

Hastings, R. P., & Brown, T. (2002). Coping strategies and the impact of challenging behaviours on special educators' burnout. *Mental Retardation, 40*(2), 148–156.

Heflin, L. J., & Alaimo, D. F. (2006). *Students with autism spectrum disorders: Effective instructional practices*. Upper Saddle River: Pearson.

Hwang, Y. S., & Kearney, P. (2013). A systematic review of mindfulness intervention for individuals with developmental disabilities: Long-term practice and long lasting effects. *Research in Developmental Disabilities, 34,* 314–326.

Hwang, Y. S., & Kearney, P. (2014). Mindful and mutual care for individuals with developmental disabilities: A systematic literature review. *Journal of Child Family Studies, 23*(3), 497–509. doi:10.1007/s10826-012-9707-9.

Idusohan-Moizer, H., Sawicka, A., Dendle, J., & Albany, M. (2013). Mindfulness-based cognitive therapy for adults with intellectual disabilities: An evaluation of the effectiveness of mindfulness in reducing symptoms of depression and anxiety. *Journal of Intellectual Disability Research,* 1–12. doi:10.1111/jir.12082.

Jackson, L., & Panyan, M. V. (2002). *Positive behavioral support in the classroom: Principles and practices*. Baltimore: Paul H Brookes.

James, N. (2013). The formal support experiences of family carers of people with an intellectual disability who also display challenging behaviour and/or mental health issues: What do carers say? *Journal of Intellectual Disabilities, 7,* 6–23.

Kabat-Zinn, J. (2003). Mindfulness-based interventions in context: Past, present, and future. *Clinical psychology: Science and Practice, 10,* 144–156.

Kaiser, A. P., & McIntyre, L. L. (2010). Introduction to special section on evidence-based practices for persons with intellectual and developmental disabilities. *American Journal on Intellectual and Developmental Disabilities, 115,* 357–363.

Kohn, A. (1993). *Punished by rewards: The trouble with gold stars, incentive plans, A's, praise, and other bribes*. Boston: Houghton Mifflin.

Kolaitis, G. (2008). Young people with intellectual disabilities and mental health needs. *Current Opinion in Psychiatry, 21,* 469–473.

Lew, M., Matta, C., Tripp-Tebo, C., & Watts, D. (2006). Dialectical behaviour therapy (DBT) for individuals with intellectual disabilities: A program description. *Mental Health Aspects of Developmental Disabilities, 9,* 1–13.

Lucyshyn, J., Albin, R., Horner, R. H., Mann, J., & Wadsworth, G. (2007). Family implementation of positive behavior support for a child with autism: Longitudinal, single-case, experimental, and descriptive replication and extension. *Journal of Positive Behavior Interventions, 9,* 131–150.

Matson, M., Mahan, S., & Matson, J. (2009). Parent training: A review of methods for children with autism spectrum disorders. *Research in Autism Spectrum Disorders, 3,* 868–875.

Mazzucchelli, T. G., & Sanders, M. R. (2011). Preventing behavioural and emotional problems in children who have a developmental disability: A public health approach. *Research in Developmental Disabilities, 32,* 2148–2156.

McGrath, A. (2013). Links between the conduct of carers and clients' challenging behaviour. *Learning Disability Practice, 16*(6), 30–32.

Miodrag, N., Lense, M. D., & Dykens, E. M. (2013). A pilot study of mindfulness intervention for individuals with Williams Syndrome: Physiological outcomes. *Mindfulness, 4,* 137–147.

Neece, C. (2013). Mindfulness-based stress reduction for parents of young children with developmental delays: Implications for parental mental health and child behaviour problems. *Journal of Applied Research in Intellectual Disabilities*. doi:10.1111/jar.12064.

Neece, C., Green, S., & Baker, B. (2012). Parenting stress and child behavior problems: A transactional relationship across time. *American Journal on Intellectual and Developmental Disabilities, 117,* 48–66.

Otis, H. G., & King, J. H. (2008). Unanticipated psychotropic medication reactions. *Journal of Mental Health Counseling, 28,* 218–240.

Pahnke, J., Lundgren, T., Hursti, T., & Hirvikoski, T. (2013). Outcomes of an acceptance and commitment therapy-based skills training group for students with high-functioning autism spectrum disorder: A quasi-experimental pilot study. *Autism*. doi:10.1177/1362361313501091

Pandita, S. U. (1993). *In this very life: The liberation teachings of the Buddha* (2nd ed.). Boston: Wisdom Publications.

Raghavan, R., & Patel, P. (2010). Ethical issues of psychotropic medication for people with intellectual disabilities. *Advances in Mental Health and Intellectual Disabilities, 4,* 34–38.

Russell, J. (2011). Mindfulness: A tool for parents and children with Asperger's syndrome. *Mindfulness, 2,* 212–215.

Sakdalan, J. A., Shaw, J., & Collier, V. (2010). Staying in the here-and-now: A pilot study on the use of dialectical behaviour therapy group skills training for forensic clients with intellectual disability. *Journal of Intellectual Disability Research, 54,* 568–572.

Segal, Z. V., Williams, J. M. G., & Teasdale, J. D. (2002). *Mindfulness-based cognitive therapy for depression: A new approach to preventing relapse*. New York: Guilford.

Shapiro, T. (2009). Psychotherapy for autism. *Journal of Infant, Child, and Adolescent Psychotherapy, 8*(1), 22–31.

Silva, L., & Schalock, M. (2012). Autism parenting stress index: Initial psychometric evidence. *Journal of Autism and Developmental Disorders, 42,* 566–574.

Singh, N. N., Wahler, R. G., Adkins, A. D., & Myers, R. E. (2003). Soles of the feet: A mindfulness-based self-control intervention for aggression by an individual with mild mental retardation. *Research in Developmental Disabilities, 24,* 158–169.

Singh, N. N., Lancioni, G. E., Winton, A. S. W., Wahler, R. G., Singh, J., & Sage, M. (2004). Mindful caregiving increases happiness among individuals with profound multiple disabilities. *Research in Developmental Disabilities, 25,* 207–218.

Singh, N. N., Lancioni, G. E., Winton, A. S. W., Curtis, W. J., Wahler, R. G., Sabaawi, M., Singh, J., & McAleavey, K. (2006a). Mindful staff increase learning and reduce aggression in adults with developmental disabilities. *Research in Developmental Disabilities, 27,* 545–558.

Singh, N. N., Lancioni, G. E., Winton, A. S. W., Fisher, B. C., Wahler, R. G., McAleavey, K., Wahler, R. G., & SaBaawi, M. (2006b). Mindful parenting decreases aggression, noncompliance, and self-injury in children with autism. *Journal of Emotional and Behavioural Disorders, 14*(3), 169–177.

Singh, N. N., Lancioni, G. E., Winton, A. S. W., Adkins, A. D., Singh, J., & Singh, A. N. (2007a). Mindfulness training assists individuals with moderate mental retardation to maintain their community placements. *Behaviour Modification, 31,* 800–814.

Singh, N. N., Lancioni, G. E., Winton, A. S. W., Singh, J., Curtis, W. J., Wahler, R. G., & McAleavey, K. M. (2007b). Mindful parenting decreases aggression and increases social behaviour in children with developmental disabilities. *Behaviour Modification, 31,* 749–771.

Singh, N. N., Lancioni, G. E., Singh, A. N., Winton, A. S. W., Singh, J., McAleavey, K., & Adkins, A. D. (2008a). A mindfulness-based health wellness program for an adolescent with Prader-Willi syndrome. *Behaviour Modification, 32,* 167–181.

Singh, N. N., Lancioni, G. E., Winton, A. S. W., Singh, A. N., Adkins, A. D., & Singh, J. (2008b). Clinical and benefit-Cost outcomes of teaching a mindfulness-based procedure to adult offenders with intellectual disabilities. *Behaviour Modification, 32,* 622–637.

Singh, N. N., Lancioni, G. E., Winton, A. S. W., Singh, A. N. A., Adkins, A. D. A., & Singh, J. (2009). Mindful staff can reduce the use of physical restraints when providing care to individuals with intellectual disabilities. *Journal of Applied Research in Intellectual Disabilities, 22,* 194–202.

Singh, N., Lancioni, G., Winton, A., Singh, J., Singh, A., Adkin, A., & Waher, R. (2010). Training in mindful caregiving transfers to parent-child interactions. *Journal of Child Family Studies, 19,* 167–174.

Singh, N. N., Lancioni, G. E., Winton, A. S. W., Singh, A. N. A., Singh, J., & Singh, A. D. A. (2011a). Effects of a mindfulness-based smoking cessation program for an adult with mild intellectual disabilitiy. *Research in Developmental Disabilities, 32,* 1180–1185.

Singh, N. N., Lancioni, G. E., Winton, A. S. W., Singh, J., Singh, A. N. A., & Singh, A. D. A. (2011b). Peer with intellectual disabilities as a mindfulness-based anger and aggression management therapist. *Research in Developmental Disabilities, 32,* 2690–2696.

Singh, N. N., Lancioni, G. E., Manikam, R., Winton, A. S. W., Singh, A. N. A., Singh, J., & Singh, A. D. A. (2011c). A mindfulness-based strategy for self-management of aggressive behaviour in adolescents with autism. *Research in Autism Spectrum Disorders, 5,* 1153–1158.

Singh, N. N., Lancioni, G. E., Singh, A. D. A., Winton, A. S. W., Singh, A. N. A., & Singh, J. (2011d). Adolescents with Asperger syndrome can use a mindfulness-based strategy to control their aggressive behaviour. *Research in Autism Spectrum Disorders, 5,* 1103–1109.

Singh, N. N., Lancioni, G. E., Winton, A. S. W., Singh, A. N., Adkins, A. D., & Singh, J. (2011e). Can adult offenders with intellectual disabilities use mindfulness-based procedures to control their deviant sexual arousal? *Psychology, Crime & Law, 17,* 165–179.

Singh, N., Lancioni, G., Karazsia, B., Winton, A., Myers, R., Singh, A. N. A., Adkins, A. D., & Singh, J. (2013a). Mindfulness-based treatment of aggession in individuals with mild intellectual disabilities: A waiting list control study. *Mindfulness, 4,* 158–167.

Singh, N., Lancioni, G., Winton, A., Karazsia, B., Singh, A. D. A., Singh, A. N. A., & Singh, J. (2013b). A mindfulness-based smoking cessation program for individuals with mild intellectual disability. *Mindfulness, 4,* 148–157.

Singh, N., Lancioni, G., Myers, R., Karazsia, B., Winton, A., & Singh, J. (2014a). A randomised controlled trial of a mindfulness-based smoking cessation program for individuals with mild intellectual disability. *International Journal of Mental Health Addiction.* doi:10.1007/s11469-013-9471-0.

Singh, N. N., Lancioni, G. E., Winton, A. S. W., Karazsia, B. T., Myers, R. E., Latham, L. I., & Singh, J. (2014b). Mindfulness-based positive behavior support (MBPBS) for mothers of adolescents with Autism Spectrum Disorder: Effects on adolescents' behavior and parental stress. *Mindfulness.* doi:10.1007/s12671-014-0321-3.

Spek, A., van Ham, N., & Nyklicek, I. (2013). Mindfulness-based therapy in adults with an autism spectrum disorder: A randomized controlled trial. *Research in Developmental Disabilities, 34*(1), 246–253.

Weiss, J. A., & Lunsky, Y. (2011). The brief family distress scale: A measure of crisis in caregivers of individuals with autism spectrum disorders. *Journal of Child Family Studies, 20,* 521–528.

Williamson, E., & Martin, A. (2012). Psychotropic medications in autism: Practical considerations for parents. *Journal of Autism and Developmental Disorders, 42,* 1249–1255.

Chapter 4
Study One: Mindfulness Intervention for Mothers

In Chap. 2, we traced the genealogy of mindfulness from its origins as *sati* in the Pāli Nikāyas to its appearance as mindfulness in contemporary psychology. We looked at how the understanding of mindfulness that came to characterise the contemporary mindfulness-based interventions (MBIs) was influenced by the work of Nyanaponika Thera and the shift that occurred after him when mindfulness came to be seen as a collective rather than a unitary term. Chapter 3 reviewed how this contemporary understanding of mindfulness has been applied in interventions for people living with developmental disabilities (DD) to ameliorate their behavioural and psychological difficulties. We have seen that MBIs may target individuals with DD directly (i.e. Category 1) by teaching them mindfulness, or indirectly (i.e. Category 2) by teaching mindfulness to their family or professional care providers. These studies have opened up new areas for investigation, for example how training in mindfulness directly affects care providers, and how their experience of mindfulness in turn influences their care recipients. Another question to be addressed concerns how mindfulness pedagogy can be adapted to meet the unique needs of individuals with DD, especially those with autism spectrum disorder (ASD), by training both their care providers and the individuals with DD themselves.

In this chapter, we focus on how this current intervention has trained six mothers of children with ASD and challenging behaviour in mindfulness theory and practice, in order to provide them with fluency in mindfulness for themselves and to equip them to act as mindfulness teachers of their own children. This intervention was carried out in two stages, where stage 1 provided mindfulness training to mothers of six children with ASD and challenging behaviours and stage 2 provided parent-mediated mindfulness training to the children themselves. This intervention had three purposes: (1) to train parents of children with ASD and challenging behaviours in mindfulness and evaluate its direct effects on them (i.e. mindfulness, parenting stress and family quality of life) and its indirect effects on their child (i.e. challenging behaviours), (2) to train parents of children with ASD and challenging behaviours to become mindfulness teachers of their own children and (3) to investigate the effects of parent-mediated mindfulness training for children with ASD and challenging behaviours. This chapter addresses the first two purposes,

Y.-S. Hwang, P. Kearney, *A Mindfulness Intervention for Children with Autism Spectrum Disorder*, Mindfulness in Behavioral Health,
DOI 10.1007/978-3-319-18962-8_4

and the third will be addressed in the next chapter. To contextualise the results of Inclusive Mindfulness (IM) training on the mothers, we will discuss the rationale behind the development and delivery of the IM programme for mother participants. In sum, this chapter addresses four issues: (1) the theoretical framework of the IM programme for mothers, (2) development of the IM programme, (3) delivery of the IM programme and (4) the results of learning and practising the IM programme.

4.1 Theoretical Framework of the Inclusive Mindfulness (IM) Programme for Mothers

4.1.1 A New Programme

The contemporary movement to apply mindfulness to the physical and psychological problems that characterise modern life began with mindfulness-based stress reduction (MBSR), developed by Jon Kabat-Zinn in the late 1970s as a secular approach to Buddhist meditation that could be used in clinical settings. The success of MBSR has inspired the development of a number of other MBIs, including mindfulness-based cognitive therapy (MBCT), acceptance and commitment therapy (ACT) and dialectical behavioural therapy (DBT), although MBSR still provides perhaps the most commonly accepted understanding of mindfulness among contemporary MBIs.

When we considered using the MBSR programme in this intervention, we were faced with two difficulties that were based on the distinctive aim of this programme, which is to train mothers to become mindfulness teachers of their own children. The first difficulty is that MBSR was designed as a stress reduction programme. While stress reduction is crucial for the support of family and professional care providers of individuals with DD, our project is not a stress reduction programme but a practitioner-teacher training programme. IM is designed to train parents to become mindfulness teachers of their own children. This is a very different purpose from that of MBSR and requires a different kind of approach. Further, we could not consider adapting MBSR to this new purpose because the practices that make up MBSR constitute a structural integrity that would be compromised by any changes in the practices themselves (McCown, Reibel, & Micozzi, 2011).

The second difficulty concerns the fact that since these mothers were to teach mindfulness to their own children, their training needed to be compatible with the kind of training they would be expected to provide for their children. To train these mothers in mindfulness in one way and then expect them to teach their children in another way would create unnecessary complications. This would exclude MBSR if only because it requires extended periods of formal meditation practice for its participants. While the parents in this intervention could fruitfully undergo such training, they could not simply reproduce this requirement for their children. This particular cohort of children is characterised by a wide range in attention span and stability, and their training activities would have to be brief, concrete, engaging and activity based.

Hence we decided to create our own training programme, designed to suit the specific requirements of our participants. We wanted an intervention that would allow mothers to become sufficiently independent in their understanding and practice of mindfulness meditation such that they could become teachers for their own children. This meant that the mothers had to do more than learning how to reproduce one or more meditation techniques. They needed the independence that comes from learning the underlying principles of mindfulness meditation and how to apply these principles to themselves and to those close to them.

To create such a programme we decided to go back to the source of mindfulness and mindfulness training, the teachings of the Buddha as recorded in the Nikāyas. We have seen in Chap. 2 how the Buddha treated *sati* as a unitary term that, while retaining its own identity, does not function alone but supported by and associated with other qualities. For example, in the training model of the eightfold path, mindfulness works intimately with effort/energy (*vāyāma*) and concentration (*samādhi*), along with all the other path factors (Bodhi, 1994). The contemporary understanding of mindfulness sees it as a collective term, one that contains its supporting qualities. For example, Kabat-Zinn (2003) has provided a definition of mindfulness that sees it as containing awareness, attention, intentionality and a specific kind of attitude, that of non-judgementality.

This shift in meaning may affect the fineness of the theoretical and practical analysis of mindfulness, and from this the adaptability of mindfulness practice to various contexts. For example, sometimes in mindfulness practice judgement is best left alone, especially when the practitioner tends to be caught in patterns of rumination associated with negative self-judgements (Segal, Williams, & Teasdale, 2002). However, sometimes judgement is an important part of mindfulness practice, for example when the practitioner wants to understand how a given mental quality can be either cultivated or abandoned, depending on its ethical character (Satipaṭṭhāna Sutta *Establishments of mindfulness*, MN 10).

In seeing mindfulness as a collective term, it is possible that the precision and flexibility of the Buddha's understanding of *sati* and its applications could be obscured. A given concept of mindfulness that works well in one context may not be applicable to another without changing the concept itself in some way. Further, it becomes more difficult, in analysis, to disentangle mindfulness itself from its supporting qualities when those qualities are seen as an inherent part of its identity. In contrast, staying with the Buddha's theoretical framework may allow for a degree of creativity in adapting mindfulness practice to suit the unique circumstances of different populations of practitioners without affecting the core meaning of the concept. We will now take a brief look at the theoretical framework that underlies the Buddha's applications of mindfulness, so we will be better placed to adapt mindfulness and its practice to contemporary conditions.

We must emphasise that in adopting this approach in this project, we were not teaching "Buddhism" to the participants. We treat the Buddha as we would any philosopher or psychologist who had something useful and relevant to say about the nature of the human condition, and who contributes, in particular, a unique set of skills in attention training. We treat the Buddha's teaching as a dharma, a concept introduced in Chap. 2 as a systematic understanding of the nature of reality (Gethin, 1998), and we saw how the various streams of psychology that came to adapt the practice of mindfulness to their own ends all came to mindfulness through the logic of their own particular dharmas. Here, we are treating the Buddha's dharma in the same critical spirit as any other.

4.1.2 The Buddha's Framework

The Buddha can be seen philosophically as an empiricist and phenomenologist (Gowans, 2003; Kalupahana, 1969, 1992), but one who differs from the European empirical tradition in that he regards the mind as another sense sensitivity, along with the five physical senses. Like the other senses, the mind (*mano*) has its own unique range of sense data (Mahāvedalla Sutta *The greater dialectic,* MN 43), these being the mental phenomena (*dhammā*) sensed by it. My eyes, for example, see the contents of this room. These sense objects are forms (*rūpa*). When I close my eyes, I can imagine the contents of this room. These sense objects are mental phenomena.

The Buddha's phenomenology is expressed in a "*dhamma* theory" (Karunadasa, 1996) that analyses the world of human experience into its constituent phenomenological parts and assembles these parts into new, systemic wholes. In this approach, the unit of experience is a *dhamma,* or dharma, where a dharma is a phenomenon or experienced event (Kalupahana, 1969, 1988; Warder, 1980). Take, for example, the objective fact of a glass of water standing on my desk. Normally I regard this glass of water as an object that exists independently of me as an experiencing subject. When I leave the room, the glass is still there, sitting on my desk. It has its own independent existence. The glass of water can also be taken as a series of dharmas, the phenomenological facts of its being seen, touched and tasted. As a phenomenon, the glass of water requires my participation, for when I turn away from it, it ceases. As an independent object, the existence of the glass of water does not depend upon me; it does not cease when I turn away from it. The Buddha is not interested in the glass of water as an independent object, but only as an experienced event as directly encountered by the experiencing subject.

The world the Buddha is interested in is not the independently existing world we normally take for granted as being out there, independent of us. Rather, he is interested in the world-as-experienced, or our-experience-of-the-world. He maps this world in great detail. For example, once recognised as a flow of dharmas, the experience of the glass of water can be subdivided according to the level of analysis required. "Seeing" is a dharma; "wanting" is a dharma; "reaching" is a dharma; "touching" is a dharma; "lifting" is a dharma; "tasting" is a dharma; "satisfaction" is a dharma; and so on. Once analysed into dharmas, the causal or conditional relationships between these dharmas can be mapped. Wanting, which is mental, conditions reaching, which is physical, while tasting, which is physical, conditions satisfaction, which is mental. For the Buddha, these represent causally connected events within which mind (e.g. wanting) conditions body (e.g. reaching), and body (e.g. tasting) conditions mind (e.g. satisfaction). All of these events and the relationships between them are available to direct experience.

Depending on his particular purpose, the Buddha analyses dharmas and the conditional relationships between them into a variety of systems. Take the immediacy of experience itself, which the Buddha calls contact (*phassa*). For the Buddha, all experience comes about through the meeting of a sense sensitivity (e.g. the eye, or visual sensitivity), its corresponding object (e.g. forms) and their corresponding awareness (e.g. visual awareness). Arising with contact is feeling (*vedanā*), which comes in the three basic flavours of pleasant (*sukha*), painful (*dukkha*) and neither-painful-nor-pleasant (*a-dukkha-(m)a-sukha*) (Madhupiṇḍika Sutta *The sweet essence,* MN 18). In brief, at even its most fundamental level, experience presents as an already complex system made up of discrete phenomena that combine in regular patterns. Remove any one phenomenon and the experienced event will not occur.

For example, as I am driving my car my eyes are struck by the visual data of the street, but because awareness is preoccupied with my thoughts, visual awareness does not arise and at that moment I do not perceive the street—and am in danger of an accident. If any of these phenomena that create and sustain this situation change, however, the experienced event transforms. If a sudden movement attracts my attention, for example, awareness then registers the traffic stopping for a red light, and I feel my focus switching from thinking to driving.

As mental and physical phenomena—dharmas—come and go into awareness, experience moves along different trajectories and life changes correspondingly. For example, the three elements that together make up a visual event may combine with pleasant feeling, and experience proceeds along a trajectory dominated by some form of desire (*lobha*). If, however, pleasant feeling is substituted by painful feeling within this complex event, then experience changes course and proceeds along a new trajectory, this one dominated by some form of aversion (*dosa*). One kind of experienced event ceases, and another takes its place.

This vision of human experience as inherently complex, dynamic and contingent has profound consequences for the therapeutic applications of meditation, for if all experience is contingent then any experience can be shaped into something else, given appropriate conditions. How it is shaped depends on our capacity to discover the causal or conditional trajectories that can send a given experienced situation into a particular direction, whether healthy (*kusala*) or unhealthy (*akusala*).

The Buddha's dharma theory provides the framework that IM draws upon to develop an approach to teaching mindfulness practice. IM is not based on the simple reproduction of a given technique, but on cultivating a living understanding of how the different elements that make up mindfulness practice can be assembled and adapted to suit the individuality of each mother and, in particular, of her child with ASD and challenging behaviours. IM is designed to teach mothers how to systematically investigate the nature of their own experience and so to uncover the dynamics that enable their mindfulness practice to develop. This in turn allows mothers to creatively adapt what they have learned to suit the unique circumstances of their children.

4.2 Development of the IM Programme

4.2.1 Training Attention

The IM programme emerges from the traditional meditation training of the second author and his experience in teaching *satipaṭṭhāna,* or mindfulness meditation, to audiences in Australia and Asia. Translating an approach to Buddhist meditation practice acquired in a traditional Buddhist society such as Burma to a contemporary non-Buddhist audience in Australia required a re-examination of the foundations of the practice. In Burma, meditation practice is part of a faith-based project to attain the state of awakening taught by the Buddha (Jordt, 2007). In Australia, meditation functions more as an open investigation into the nature of experience within a secular, even scientific context (Higgins, 2012; McMahan, 2008).

Investigation, however, is common to both the traditional and contemporary approaches to mindfulness meditation, and the tradition closely associates mindfulness and investigation (Bodhi, 2005; Pandita, 1993). IM adapts traditional mindfulness meditation practice to the contemporary world by presenting it as the objective study of one's own subjective experience. When introducing the very concept of "meditation" to his audiences, the second author defines it as the systematic training of attention.

The practice of attention, *manasikāra* in Pāli, lies at the heart of both the Buddha's approach to meditation and to IM. The Buddha spoke in particular of *yoniso manasikāra,* traditionally translated as proper, wise or methodical attention (Nyanatiloka, 1980; Rhys Davids & Stede, 1999), and more recently as careful attention (Bodhi, 2012) and appropriate attention (Thanissaro, 1996). We are reminded of Nyanaponika Thera's concept of "bare attention" as summing up the central activity of *satipaṭṭhāna* (Thera, 1969). When we consider what traditional meditation practice has brought to contemporary Western society, we suggest that its distinctive contribution lies in the very idea of systematically and objectively attending to one's own subjective experience, supported by a practical technology to accomplish that endeavour. Mindfulness, in other words, is one part of an attentional stance that can be applied to different contexts, both individual and social. The role of mindfulness is to apply memory to attention. The mindful person *remembers* to attend to the object of awareness. Mindfulness therefore functions to "keep the object always in view, neither forgetting it nor allowing it to disappear" (Pandita, 1993, p. 100).

4.2.2 Inclusive Mindfulness

Our approach to mindfulness training is inclusive, in that it is designed to be sufficiently adaptable to allow those with disabilities to participate in mindfulness training to whatever degree they find possible. The quality of inclusivity is a natural extension of the nature of the Buddha's framework of dependent arising, where reality is not fixed but inherently fluid and contingent. This understanding suggests that every situation is workable and that the practice of mindfulness can be adapted to whatever particular combination of sensitivities and insensitivities characterises a given population. Mindfulness practice, for example, consists of tracking the flow of experience over time, regardless of the object of experience. While certain objects of attention, such as breathing, have been popular in the past, and certain attentional techniques, such as maintaining a sitting posture over a period of time, have been hallowed by tradition, mindfulness practice itself is not dependent on any specific object of attention or technique (Gethin, 2001). Any aspect of experience may serve as an entry point for the continuity of awareness, provided only that the practitioner is sufficiently sensitive to it for him or her to maintain awareness on it. As the sensitivity of individual practitioners differs, so the objects of attention suitable for those individuals may vary, and the techniques they employ to maintain their attention may vary.

The second author has found that any given population of practitioners will include some who cannot fruitfully use the objects and techniques provided by standardised meditation methods, but that every person has a sensitivity that can provide an entry into the depths of their experience. In practical pedagogical terms, it is just a matter of finding it. For this project, we have attempted to adapt the first principles of mindfulness practice to suit the needs and abilities of the particular population with whom we are working, the mothers of children with ASD and challenging behaviours, along with the children themselves. Hence, we have named this approach to mindfulness practice Inclusive Mindfulness (IM).

4.2.3 Serenity and Insight

The basic structure of mindfulness practice was presented to the mothers as: (1) settle awareness in the body and (2) see what happens. The Buddha speaks of meditation practice as entailing two basic qualities, serenity (*samatha*) and insight (*vipassanā*). The practitioner needs both. The Buddha explains that some practitioners may develop serenity but not insight, while others may develop insight but not serenity. The practitioner begins by cultivating the stronger quality, but at some point should then develop the weaker quality, so that both are strong and balanced (Samādhi Sutta *Concentration (3),* AN 4:94). Serenity indicates the affective aspect of meditation. It allows the heart (*citta*) to be steadied, composed, unified and concentrated. Insight indicates the cognitive aspect of meditation. It allows experienced events (*saṅkhārā*) to be seen, explored and "insighted" (*vipassati*).

Experience has shown that some degree of serenity is needed if the practitioner's mind is to become sufficiently settled to begin to see clearly what is happening within their body and mind, and the body is frequently used as the basis for serenity practice. In the four establishments of mindfulness, for example, body (*kāya*) is listed first, and is generally taken to constitute the starting point of the practice because it is the most obvious of the four (Anālayo, 2006).

Settling awareness in the body entails using mindfulness immersed in body (*kāyagatā sati*) to ground the practitioner in body awareness (Kāyagatāsati Sutta

Mindfulness immersed in body, MN 119). Body awareness brings the practitioner to the present and counters distracting thoughts, thus stimulating serenity. *Seeing what happens* entails investigating the gradual unfolding of previously unnoticed details and patterns of experience that naturally become apparent once the mind is settled on present experience, thus stimulating insight (*vipassanā*). As mindfulness develops, practitioners become increasingly sensitive to the details and flows of human experience (Anālayo, 2006; Gunaratana, 1985; Kuan, 2008).

4.3 Delivery of the IM Programme

4.3.1 The Intervention

The IM programme for six mothers comprised eight weekly sessions with a four-week break between the seventh and eighth sessions. The break provided mother participants with the opportunity to practise independently and report back their experience, and functioned as a transition to a two-month self-practice period. This arrangement was to prepare each mother to teach mindfulness to her own child (stage 2). Intervention meetings were held on Saturdays at a suburban yoga studio and lasted two and a half hours.

Each session introduced a particular theme that was presented through a guided meditation offered as a practice experiment, expanded on by readings provided by the second author. The themes allowed for a gradual development of the theory and practice of mindfulness meditation covering both body (e.g. breathing) and mind (e.g. feeling and thinking). A guided meditation session, presented as a practice experiment, was followed by open discussion in which mothers were encouraged to reflect back on their meditation experience, describing it for others and asking questions about it.

The sessions opened with a discussion of participants' experience of their mindfulness practice from the previous meeting, and of their daily lives as mothers of children with ASD and challenging behaviours. The mothers quickly became very open with each other about their experience, and in discussion with the teachers they learned to place the particularities of their everyday and meditation experience into the general framework of the Buddha's understanding of the mind.

The opening discussion was followed by a period of stretching exercises to relax and prepare body and mind for mindfulness practice. The aim was to help them develop a posture in which they could be comfortably still for a period of between 20 and 30 min of formal practice.

After each formal meditation exercise, the teachers led a discussion regarding the experiences that mothers underwent during their formal practice. These discussions were supported by the practice by each participant of writing an individual reflective diary on their mindfulness practice, including formal mindfulness sessions and mindfulness in everyday activities. Through discussions and writings, mothers were encouraged to become curious about the nature of their experience as it unfolded, and then investigate it thoroughly with complete trust in whatever they uncovered. Mothers were enabled to develop the sensitivity and the language necessary to allow subjective experience to emerge as inter-subjective understanding, and their meditation experiences, no matter how strange they seemed at the time, were normalised through this process. The more they learned to communicate the details of their experience, the more fluent they became in discovering what they had not noticed before, and the more normalised their experiences became. In this way, the mothers were able to grow in confidence regarding their mindfulness practice, and to become more assured in their reading of the state of their own minds and communicating it to others.

In addition, during their training mothers were asked to keep a record of their child's challenging behaviour to enhance their understanding of its nature, function and frequencies. This practice was to support mothers to deepen their insight into their child's behaviour. Additional learning supports included a website containing weekly readings in both written document and audio file formats to suit their individual learning needs, and guided meditations in an audio file format. However, the most crucial support came from the mothers themselves. From their first meeting, the mothers formed a social bond that transformed a meditation class into a closely linked social support network. The passionate discussions that characterised each meeting covered the joys and sorrows of raising children with ASD and the ways in which mindfulness meditation might help them.

Since the aim of the training was to train each mother to become a mindfulness teacher for her own child, we emphasised two aspects of training: nurturing independence through the empirical investigation of different aspects of experience and strengthening the capacity to communicate the experiences elicited by this training using the triad-training model (Fig. 4.1). This model consists of maintaining a balance between experiential and cognitive learning, between individual and collective learning, and between everyday and formal practice.

The details of the programme are presented below and are summarised in Table 4.1 *Theory and practice of the IM programme.*

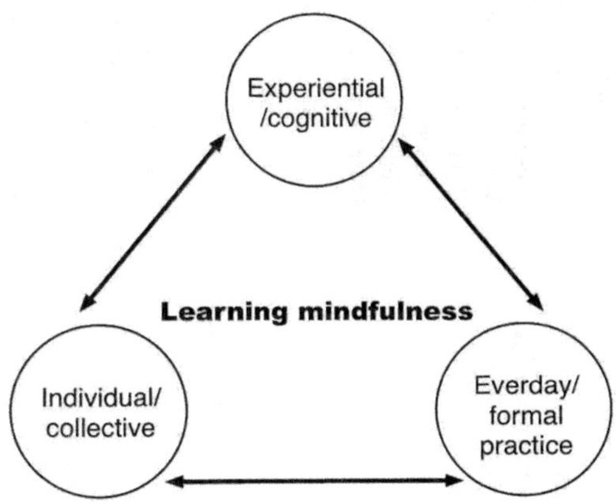

Fig. 4.1 Triad-training model of mindfulness

Table 4.1 Theory and practice of the IM programme

Weekly theme	Topics and activities	Objectives	Sources	Reading
1. Introducing mindfulness	Pre-training exercises What is mindfulness? What is meditation? Loosening and relaxing Meditation posture Overview of IM	Getting to know parents and their children; identifying motivations Introduction to mindfulness meditation practice; stimulating interest and curiosity Loosening and relaxing participants; introducing meditation posture Continue momentum in mindfulness training	(Kabat-Zinn, 2003) (Bodhi, 2000) (Satipaṭṭhāna Sutta *The establishments of mindfulness*, MN 10) (Sekha Sutta *The trainee*, MN 53) (Mahāsīhanāda Sutta *Greater discourse of the lion's roar,* MN 12) (Saṅgārava Sutta *To Saṅgārava*, SN 47:55)	Introducing mindfulness
2. Serenity and insight	Concepts of serenity and insight Loosening and relaxing Structuring attention Relationships to the meditation object Meditation on elements	Understanding of serenity and insight Loosening and relaxing participants; Learning precision in attention, by exercising aim supported by naming Developing understanding of the elements of applying attention Continue momentum in mindfulness training	(Mahā-Assapura Sutta *The greater discourse at Assapura,* MN 39) (Saṅgārava Sutta *To Saṅgārava,* SN 47:55) (Sedaka Sutta, *At Sedaka* SN 47:19) (Tatiya Samādhi Sutta *Concentration (3),* AN 4:94) (Bāla Vagga *Fools*, AN 2:31) (Thera, 1969) (Mahasi, 1971)	Serenity and insight
3. Tracking breathing	Concept of dharma Loosening and relaxing Breathing as a meditation object Walking meditation	Clarifying understanding of mindfulness practice as presented so far Loosening and relaxing participants Learning to find more detail and interest in routine movements of breathing Learning basics of walking meditation Continue momentum in mindfulness training	(Kalupahana, 1992) (Karunadasa, 1996) (Pandita, 1993) (Sabba Sutta *On everything,* SN 4.15) (Satipaṭṭhāna Sutta *The establishments of mindfulness,* MN 10) Ānāpānasati Sutta *Mindfulness through breathing,* MN 118) (Mahāhattipadopama Sutta *Greater discourse on the simile of elephant's footprint,* MN 28)	Discerning elements

Table 4.1 (continued)

Weekly theme	Topics and activities	Objectives	Sources	Reading
4. Tracking feeling	Concept of vedanā ("feeling") Loosening and relaxing Exploring "watching" and "feeling"	Clarifying understanding of mindfulness practice as presented so far Understanding of vedanā Loosening and relaxing participants Exploring the difference between "watching" and "feeling" Continue momentum in mindfulness training	(Anālayo, 2006) (Satipaṭṭhāna Sutta *The establishments of mindfulness,* MN 10) (Cūḷavedalla Sutta *The lesser dialectic,* MN 44) (Madhupiṇḍika Sutta *The sweet essence,* MN 18)	Clear understanding On feeling
5. Tracking the thought-stream	Using thinking as a meditation object Loosening and relaxing Practising mindfulness in movement	Clarifying understanding of mindfulness practice as presented so far Loosening and relaxing participants Learning to treat thought as just another meditation object Continue momentum in mindfulness training	(Dennett, 1991) (Maharaj, 1998) (Satipaṭṭhāna Sutta *The establishments of mindfulness,* MN 10) (Salla Sutta *The arrow,* SN 36:6) (Vassakāra Sutta *To Vassakāra,* AN 4:35)	The Thought-stream
6. The sublime states	Introducing the sublime states (brahmā vihāra) and meditation to cultivate them Loosening and relaxing	Clarifying understanding of mindfulness practice as presented so far Loosening and relaxing participants Introduction to mood-induction meditation Continue momentum in mindfulness training	(Karaṇīya Mettā Sutta *How mettā is to be done,* Khp 9) (Rāja Sutta *The king,* Ud 5.1) (Kālāma Sutta *To the Kālāmas*, AN 3:65) (Mettā Sutta *On mettā,* AN 11:15) (Dhānañjāni Sutta *To Dhānañjāni,* MN 97)	The sublime states
7. Finding the balance	Clear understanding and its role in meditation Cultivating reflexive awareness Refining meditation by balancing the mental factors of right energy (vāyāma), mindfulness (sati) and unification (samādhi)	Clarifying understanding of mindfulness practice as presented so far Cultivating reflexive awareness Learning to communicate practice experience, using (right) energy, mindfulness and unification as framework Continue momentum in mindfulness training	(Thera, 1969) (Anālayo, 2006) (Thera, 1987) (Satipaṭṭhāna Sutta *The establishments of mindfulness,* MN 10) (Mahācattārīsaka Sutta *The great forty,* MN 117) (Saṅgārava Sutta *To Saṅgārava,* SN 46:55)	Finding the balance

Table 4.1 (continued)

Weekly theme	Topics and activities	Objectives	Sources	Reading
8. The four truths	Loosening and relaxing Four truths (cattāro ariya-saccāni) as a framework for understanding the nature of practice Learning to communicate practice experience Plans for the future of the project	Clarifying understanding of mindfulness practice as presented so far Loosening and relaxing participants Learning to communicate practice experience; weaving the four truths into discussion; classical and contemporary approaches Clarifying plans for the future of the project	(Dhammacakkappavattana Sutta *Turning the dharma wheel,* SN 56:11) (Satipaṭṭhāna Sutta *The establishments of mindfulness,* MN 10) (Sabbāsava Sutta *All the taints,* MN 2) (Mahāvedalla Sutta *The greater dialectic,* MN 43)	The four truths

4.3.2 *The Weekly Sessions*

4.3.2.1 Week One: Introducing Mindfulness

Prior to the formal beginning of training, mothers were asked to choose a routine daily activity such as washing dishes, vacuuming the floor or driving a car and then try to keep their attention on the activity continuously. This meant noticing how often their awareness would slip away, and how difficult it is to maintain attention on a single activity over a period of time. At the first meeting, this exercise was used as an entry to understanding the concept of mindfulness as memory and meditation as the systematic training of attention.

Participants were given instructions in setting up a sitting or supine posture, and a stretching session helped them relax. A formal guided meditation followed, using the basic instructions to *settle awareness in the body* and then *see what happens*. Discussion followed, where participants were encouraged to develop the view that whatever happened to them during meditation *is* meditation, and is correct. Throughout the session, mothers were encouraged to be interested and curious about their experience and how it unfolds. Finally, participants were encouraged to continue their practice and, in particular, to practise mindfulness in a chosen daily activity.

4.3.2.2 Week Two: Serenity and Insight

This and all subsequent sessions began with open discussion of the meditation homework and any other issues the mothers found relevant. These quickly became vibrant discussions in which mothers shared openly with each other. In this meeting they were then given further instructions in the meditation method, including the distinction between serenity and insight and the importance of maintaining an attitude of open investigation and playfulness in their practice. The very idea of creating a meditation method by structuring attention was introduced and developed, filling out the original instructions of *settle awareness in the body* and then *see what happens*. In particular, the subject of distraction was introduced, and participants were encouraged to become interested in it so that distraction itself could become a meditation object.

The formal meditation exercise entailed tracking the elemental qualities of physical experience, learning to precisely aim awareness at specific sensations throughout the body. This practice assisted participants to ground their awareness in the body and to learn to aim awareness precisely at a chosen physical sensation and then communicate what happens as a result.

4.3.2.3 Week Three: Tracking Breathing

This session introduced the practice of walking meditation, learning to track the movement of the body and the touch of the feet on the floor as one moves. Walking meditation was presented as a way to bring mindfulness practice into everyday life, as the body moves from one activity to another. In the guided meditation session, the emphasis was on tracking breathing. A series of attention exercises directed the awareness of the mothers to the specific details of the breathing process. Drawing upon the tracking of the elements practised in week two, participants were encouraged to directly experience the elemental qualities of breathing, without being caught up in their concepts about their breathing.

Another theme introduced with this practice was that of the primacy of experience, that mindfulness practice is not concerned with what one believes, but what and how one experiences. Hence, the practitioner learns to doubt the validity of habitual perceptions and judgements and instead look for the direct sensation as it arises in the present.

4.3.2.4 Week Four: Tracking Feeling

The concept of clear understanding (*sampajañña*) was introduced in the formal teaching, as the intelligence that emerges when we track our experience over time. We begin to become aware of our normal habitual patterns, and how they are conditioned. We also become aware of the patterns of those close to us, and attention was drawn to the fact that mothers were already noticing new aspects of their children's behaviour.

The concept and practice of feeling (*vedanā*) was introduced in the guided meditation. Feeling was introduced as a mode of experiencing, and practitioners experimented with the difference between watching breathing and feeling breathing. The subject of feeling raised that of cultivating intimacy in our experience, learning to become closer to actual experience rather than being separated by our habitual concepts about our experience.

4.3.2.5 Week Five: Tracking the Thought Stream

The focus in this session was learning to use thinking as a meditation object. This practice is important for those who are distracted by thinking as it allows them to recognise that any distraction, no matter how severe, can become an object of mindfulness. In a daily life context, we may become obsessed with our perceived problems and stresses by obsessively thinking about them. Treating thought as simply another object of mindfulness allows the practitioner to cut through these obsessions, and to become aware of the underlying emotional state that feeds the thinking—and then to track that emotion as a meditation object.

Mothers were given a guided meditation in a number of playful exercises that included investigating questions such as "How do you know you are thinking?" (i.e. looking at how thought appears), "Where do you think?" and "What does thinking feel like?" This session also included follow-up exercises in moving meditation, learning to be mindful of the body as it moves.

4.3.2.6 Week Six: The Sublime States

This session focused on the cultivation of the four sublime states, those of love (*mettā*), compassion (*karuṇā*), joy (*muditā*) and equanimity (*upekkhā*). The training had previously emphasised insight (*vipassanā*) practice, where mothers were trained to simply investigate the nature of their current experience and understand how it flows and changes. The practice of the sublime states represented a move to serenity (*samatha*) practice, where the emphasis in the first three sublime states was on cultivating a specific mood state, that of love in its various forms. Compassion was presented as love directed towards those in pain, and joy as love directed towards those enjoying happiness. The fourth sublime state, equanimity, was presented as the balance that comes from accepting happiness and pain as natural parts of human life. Love was compared to the love of a mother for her child, compassion to love when her child is in pain, joy to love when her child is happy, and equanimity to a mother releasing her child into the world to be responsible for his or her own fate.

The practice of the sublime states was presented as an alternative to the practice of directly engaging with current experience. It was suggested that the practitioner could use this kind of practice when she wanted to take a break from directly confronting her present situation.

4.3.2.7 Week Seven: Finding the Balance

This week participants revised and deepened their understanding of clear understanding (*sampajañña*), the intelligence that accompanies and is developed by mindfulness practice. Clear understanding was presented as the development of a broader picture of how life unfolds, and drawing upon an image that originated with a participant, it was compared to a weather report of the state of one's mind. Participants learn to become sensitive to today's emotional state and to recognise what is needed to accommodate this "weather".

The formal practice presented three exercises in understanding one's inner state, in which mothers learned to modify their attentional stance so as to notice what was happening in the background of their minds. This allows the practitioner to use mindfulness as a way of cultivating awareness of the whole field of the mind and whatever is going on within it.

Finally, mindfulness practice was discussed as a project of finding a balance within the mind. The Buddha's model of meditation found in his eightfold path was presented as a working example. Here, meditation is seen as the cultivation of a balance between the active factor of energy/effort (*vāyāma*) and the peaceful, receptive quality of concentration/unification (*samādhi*), with mindfulness (*sati*) as the balancing quality. The Buddha also presents a language with which to communicate meditation experience, to oneself or to others. Finally, the reading for this session included practical meditation exercises in recognising when the mind is out of balance and what strategies might be used to bring it back into balance.

4.3.2.8 Week Eight: The Four Truths

This was the final session, conducted after a self-practice period of four weeks. The formal teaching presented the Buddha's four truths as a therapeutic model. The truths concern *dukkha* (pain, unsatisfactoriness), its arising and ceasing, and the path leading to its cessation. Through mindfulness we learn to directly face our pain, and through clear understanding we learn to understand it. Then the contingency of our pain is revealed, and the path—the possibilities contained within the situation that might provide a solution—becomes possible.

This model became the starting point for a discussion on how one's experience can be directly encountered and then communicated, both internally to oneself and externally to others. Through mindfulness practice we become intimate with our experience, both private and social, and we learn to understand how that experience flows. From this we can see what changes we need to make in our lives and sense the possibilities that our situation contains. But for this process to be effective, we must also learn how to communicate the depths and details of our experience, and the Buddha gives us a language in which to do this.

4.3.3 Participants

A total of six mother–child dyads participated in this small pilot case study. The ages of the mothers ranged between 34 and 48, and their education qualifications varied from a Technical and Further Education (TAFE) Certificate to a Post-Graduate Diploma. All child participants were diagnosed with ASD by a health professional, such as a paediatrician, psychiatrist or clinical psychologist. The ages of the children, five males and one female, ranged from 8 to 15. The challenging behaviour they exhibited included physical and verbal aggression, self-injury and breakages. All names are pseudonyms.

Molly and Casey constitute the first dyad. Molly was 37 years old and had a bachelor's degree. She participated in this study with Casey, 10 years old. He was the first son of her three children, all of whom were diagnosed with ASD. Casey's paediatrician had initially diagnosed him with pervasive developmental disorder-not otherwise specified (PDD-NOS) before his fourth birthday. Casey was spending two days a week at a special education unit attached to a mainstream primary school and three days at home receiving distance education services from Education Queensland. When he was angry and frustrated, he externalised his emotions by blaming others or objects. His challenging behaviours included yelling, screaming, hitting, kicking, spitting, licking and biting.

The second dyad is made up of Vicky and Sam. Vicky was 34 years old and had a TAFE Certificate. Sam, 10 years old, was initially diagnosed at 7 years with Asperger's syndrome by a psychiatrist, and subsequently with high functioning autism (HFA). From the age of five he received cognitive behaviour therapy (CBT) from a psychologist, and treatment continued throughout this project. At school, his challenging behaviours included yelling, throwing, hitting, kicking, punching and pinching, as expressions of his stress and anxiety. He also spoke about suicide and going to heaven. On joining the project Vicky transferred Sam to full-time home education.

Mariam and Peter constitute the third dyad. Mariam was 45 years old with a bachelor's degree. Her son, Peter, was 12 years old with multiple diagnoses. He was initially diagnosed with HFA at the age of three, and later with mild intellectual disability and Tourette's. He also had acute anxiety. He had been in a mainstream school but moved into a special school about a year before the project because of his challenging behaviours (e.g. screaming, crying, hitting his head, running away and throwing things). Peter often thought that when people around him frowned, they did so because they were angry with him. This misinterpretation added to his anxiety.

The fourth dyad is composed of Diana and her son John. Diana was 37 years old and was studying towards a bachelor's degree. John was 8 years old and placed in a mainstream primary school. A psychiatrist initially diagnosed him with Asperger's syndrome when he was three, and 2 years later a psychologist diagnosed him with PDD-NOS. John was also recognised as gifted and talented, and was thriving academically. His challenging behaviours, however, including running away, hitting, kicking, swearing and throwing things, made his school experience extremely difficult. John's paediatrician referred him to this project.

Shane and her son David constitute the fifth dyad. Shane was 48 years old and had a TAFE Certificate. David was 15 years old and had been recently diagnosed with Asperger's by a psychiatrist. He had problems with anger that manifested in his language and behaviour, including breakages (e.g. dents in walls, broken mobile phone) and self-injuries (e.g. graffiti using his own blood, bruised and swollen knuckles). He attended a mainstream secondary school. David's classroom teacher recommended he join this project, and Shane agreed as she felt she had reached a breaking point because of the escalation of the anger and stress in her household.

The last dyad consists of Sally and her daughter Bindy. Sally was 42 years old and possessed a post-graduate diploma. Bindy was 12 years old and had been diagnosed with ASD by two paediatricians before the age of four. She frequently used echolalia for communication. When frustrated, she hit her head on the wall and bit others and subsequently engaged in pinching (herself and others), kicking and biting. According to Sally, Bindy had been placed in a "behaviour room" at school with mostly preverbal students. Sally chose to participate in this study because more than anything else she wanted to address her own anger, caused by her constant struggles to raise her daughter.

No mothers had practised mindfulness prior to their engagement in this study, and two had never heard of the practice. The majority of mothers decided to participate because of recommendations made by their child's classroom teacher or paediatrician. They learned about the project through advertisements on various websites (Department of Education Queensland, Department of Communities, Child Safety and Disability Services, Autism Queensland, Autism Centre of Excellence in Griffith University) and through local psychologist and MBSR networks in Brisbane, Queensland. The Human Research Ethics Committee (HREC) of Griffith University approved this study (EDN/64/12/HREC).

4.3.4 Teacher Quality and Intervention Fidelity

Teachers play a central role in the outcomes of mindfulness interventions (Hwang & Kearney, 2013; McCown et al., 2011; Segal et al., 2002). They are responsible for delivering the intervention with accuracy and consistency while demonstrating the flexibility necessary to accommodate a wide variety of learner characteristics and learning environments. The pedagogical skills required for teaching mindfulness include the capacity to conceptualise the experiences elicited by mindfulness practice and to communicate them in an evocative and shared manner (McCown et al., 2011). These capacities form two dimensions, a theoretical and practical understanding of mindfulness on one hand, and pedagogy on the other. Teaching mindfulness to individuals living with disabilities, including both people with disabilities and their families or professional caregivers, adds additional demands. These are theoretical knowledge of the nature and educational requirements of disability, and experience in applying them in practice.

Figure 4.2 presents the three dimensions of teacher quality required in the provision of mindfulness interventions to individuals living with disabilities. The two authors formed a team that fully met these requirements. Patrick Kearney is an independent dharma teacher who has been trained in mindfulness both academically and experientially. He developed the IM programme to directly link the contemporary secular practice of mindfulness meditation to the Buddha's teachings as found in the Pāli Nikāyas. He has been practising mindfulness meditation for 40 years and teaching it for over 20 years, through groups, workshops and intensive residential retreats. The practical and theoretical understanding of mindfulness that he brought to this project was synergised with the understanding of Yoon-Suk Hwang regarding disability and teaching pedagogy. A practitioner of mindfulness for 10 years, she has been trained in teaching learners with disabilities since 1996. Her teaching and research experience in the fields of developmental disabilities contributed to the development and delivery of the IM programmes for both mothers and children.

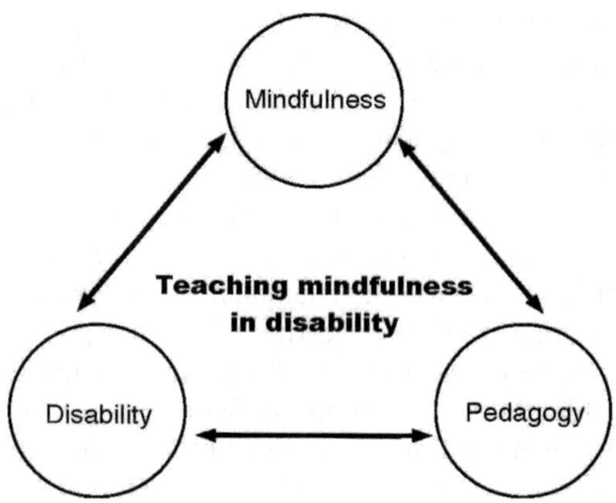

Fig. 4.2 Three dimensions of teacher quality in teaching mindfulness in disability

We adopted the following strategies to ensure intervention fidelity. First, the IM programme developers delivered the intervention. Prior to each intervention session, intervention plans were developed with learning objectives, activities and pedagogy. All intervention sessions were video-recorded and transcribed. Following Smith, Daunic and Taylor (2007), checklists for intervention fidelity were developed to monitor the accuracy and consistency of the mindfulness intervention, indicating it was implemented as planned and delivered in a comparable manner to all participants. The checklists contained 11 Yes/No questions covering five areas: study design, training fidelity, treatment delivery fidelity, treatment receipt, treatment enactment and effectiveness (Table 4.2). A researcher in psychology, who is independent of this study and familiar with mindfulness practice, examined video footages of two randomly selected mindfulness-training sessions (25 % of total sessions) and completed checklists, demonstrating 100 % intervention fidelity. In addition, no mother participant dropped out of the training.

Table 4.2 Fidelity checklists for IM programme for mothers

Fidelity area	Question	Yes	No
Study design	Does the learning objective conform to the theory/definition of mindfulness?		
Study design	Do the learning activities conform to the theory/definition of mindfulness?		
Training	Was the learning objective planned prior to the intervention?		
Training	Was the learning objective addressed during the intervention?		
Training	Were learning activities planned prior to the intervention?		
Training	Were learning activities delivered during the intervention?		
Treatment delivery	Was teaching pedagogy planned prior to the intervention?		
Treatment delivery	Was planned teaching pedagogy delivered during the intervention?		
Treatment receipt	Did the participants perform mindfulness activities during the intervention?		
Treatment enactment	Did the teachers address and monitor the importance of continuing mindfulness practice in real life settings outside the intervention settings? (Fidelity of treatment enactment)		
Effectiveness	Were the teachers flexible enough to allow for the intervention to be readily implemented in real world settings (e.g. allow participants to ask questions or make suggestions, not adhering too strictly to the plan)?		

4.3.5 Data Collection

We investigated both the direct and indirect effects of training mothers in mindfulness. The Freiburg Mindfulness Inventory, Parenting Stress Scale and the Beach Family Quality of Life Questionnaire were used to examine the direct effects of mindfulness training on mothers. The Child Behaviour Checklist was used to evaluate the indirect effects of training mothers in mindfulness on their own children with ASD and challenging behaviours. Mothers completed these questionnaires before and after the mindfulness training. They also kept a reflective diary of their own mindfulness practice to observe and monitor the details of their experience. The individual reflective diaries were transcribed for qualitative analysis along with the group discussions during the eight training sessions, where mothers collectively explored their experiences of mindfulness practice.

4.3.6 Direct Effects on Parents: Mindfulness

The short form of the Freiburg Mindfulness Inventory (Walach, Buchheld, Buttenmuller, Kleinknecht, & Schmidt, 2006) was used to examine the level of mindfulness in parents. This inventory has 14 mindfulness-related items on a four-point Likert scale, ranging from rarely to almost always. It demonstrates high reliability (0.86).

4.3.7 Direct Effects on Parents: Parenting Stress

Parenting stress was also investigated. The Parenting Stress Scale (Berry & Jones, 1995) was used to investigate the feelings and perceptions surrounding the experience of parenting. This self-report scale contains 18 items concerning relationships with children rated on a five-point Likert scale, ranging from strongly disagree (1) to strongly agree (5) with a possible range between 18 and 90. It has shown high internal reliability (0.83) and test–retest reliability (0.81) (Berry & Jones, 1995).

4.3.8 Direct Effects on Parents: Family Quality of Life

The Beach Family Quality of Life (FQoL) scale was developed to assess the quality of life of families of children with disabilities (Hoffman, Marquis, Poston, Summers, & Turnbull, 2006). It consists of five subscales (i.e. family interaction, parenting, emotional wellbeing, physical/material wellbeing and disability-related support) rated on a five-point scale, ranging from very dissatisfied to very satisfied. High reliability and validity have been reported for FQoL (Hoffman et al., 2006). For example, Cronbach's alpha for the subscales on importance ratings was 0.94 and on satisfaction ratings was 0.88.

4.3.9 *Indirect Effects on Children: Challenging Behaviours*

The Child Behaviour Checklist (CBCL Achenbach & Rescorla, 2001) was adopted to investigate parents' perceptions of children's behaviour in family contexts. The CBCL for ages 6–18 consists of 113 items on a three-point Likert scale, ranging between 0 (not true) and 2 (very true or often true). Because of its good scale reliability and validity, the CBCL has been used by other studies (e.g. Oord, Bögels, & Peijnenburg, 2012) to demonstrate the effects of mindfulness practice on children in mental health care.

4.3.10 *Data Analysis*

Quantitative data were analysed using the statistical package for the social sciences (SPSS v21). Due to the study's small sample size, the nonparametric paired-sample Wilcoxon signed rank test was used to assess differences between pre- and post-mindfulness parent training. For the qualitative data analysis, the training sessions with mothers were transcribed verbatim from video recordings. Guided by an inductive thematic analysis approach (Braun & Clarke, 2006), qualitative analysis began with generating initial codes, naming interesting segments of data that characterised mothers' experience of meditation, and searching for themes that allowed the data extracts to form coherent patterns. NVivo 8 software was used for data management and coding. The next sections detail the effects of mindfulness parent training with a focus on the quantitative analysis results. In the current chapter and in Chap. 5, qualitative data will be used, wherever appropriate, to contextualise quantitative analysis results. They shed light on the nature of the effects of mindfulness parent training, along with their developmental trajectories.

4.4 Results of IM Programme

4.4.1 *Direct Effects on Mothers*

Figure 4.3 presents the raw data from the mothers before and after mindfulness training (i.e. the initial and final scores for each mother) regarding levels of mindfulness, parenting stress and quality of family life. Regarding mindfulness, the direct focus of the intervention, five mothers showed an increase and one (Molly) maintained her initial level. A paired-sample Wilcoxon signed rank test confirmed the overall increase in the level of mindfulness was significant ($z=-2.032$, $N=6$, $p=0.042$). Regarding parenting stress, five mothers demonstrated a reduction, while one mother (Molly) showed a slight increase. This result translated into a paired-sample Wilcoxon signed rank result that was not statistically significant ($z=-1.682$, $n=6$,

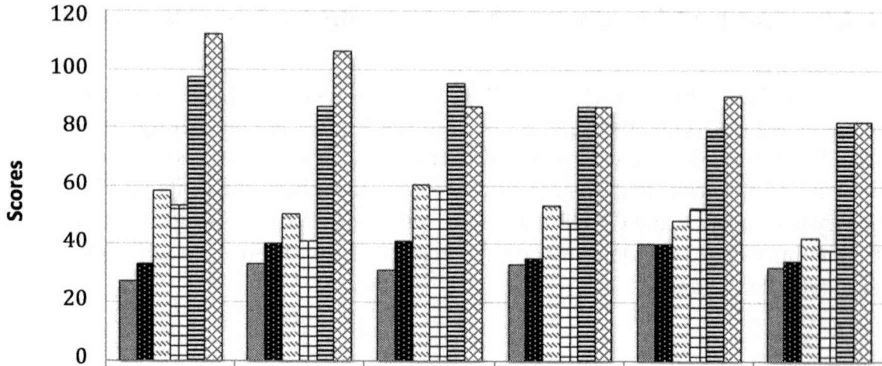

	Vicky	Diana	Mariam	Shane	Molly	Sally
MI_Pre	27	33	30.6	33	40	32
MI_Post	33	40	41	35	40	34
PSS_Pre	58	50	60	53	48	42
PSS_Post	53	41	58	47	52	38
QoL_Pre	97	87	95	87	79	82
QoL_Post	112	106	87	87	91	82

Fig. 4.3 Direct effects of the parent mindfulness training on mothers

$p=0.093$). Given the small number in the study, it is possible that Molly's increased stress may have contributed to this absence of statistical significance. The results for quality of family life after the mindfulness training were variable, with three mothers (Molly, Vicky and Diana) showing noticeable increases, two (Shane and Sally) showing no difference and Mariam showing a reduction. A group analysis of family quality of life yielded no statistically meaningful difference.

4.4.2 Indirect Effects on Children

The CBCL was used to examine the indirect effects of parent mindfulness training on their children with ASD and challenging behaviours. It consists of nine subscales: (1) anxious/depressed, (2) withdrawn/depressed, (3) somatic complaints, (4) social problems, (5) thought problems, (6) attention problems, (7) rule-breaking behaviour, (8) aggressive behaviour and (9) other problems. CBCL Total Problems Scores are recommended to assess any changes resulting from an intervention (Achenbarch & Rescorla, 2001).

Figure 4.4 presents CBCL scores for the six children before and after the parent mindfulness intervention. All children, except Molly's son, Casey, demonstrated reductions in their Total Problem scores. Reductions in Sam and David's Total Problem scores were particularly noticeable. Before the intervention their Total Problem scores were 101, representing the highest score, and at the conclusion of the parent mindfulness training their scores were 54 and 77 respectively, down by 47 and 24.

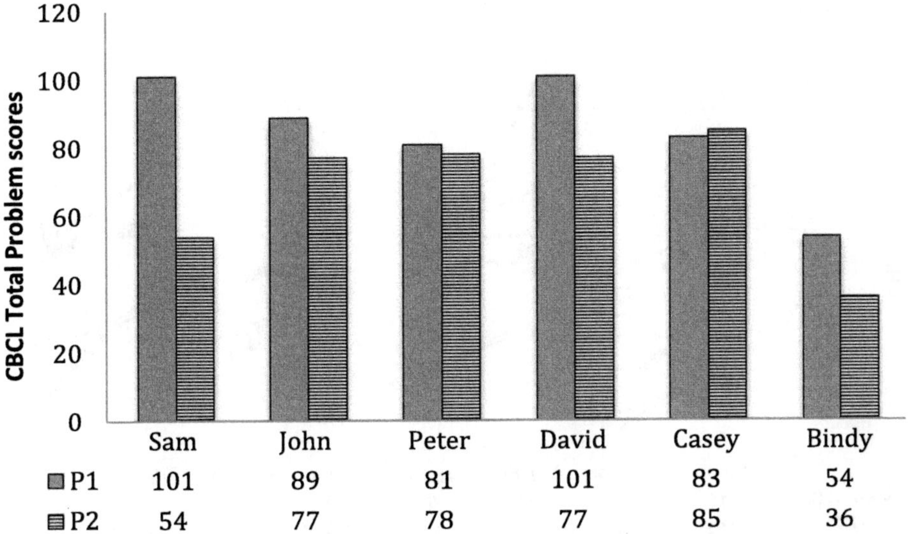

Fig. 4.4 CBCL total problems scores before and after the parent mindfulness training

After the parent mindfulness intervention the Total Problem scores reported for John and Bindy were 77 and 36, down from 89 and 54 prior to the intervention. The initial Total Problem scores of Peter and Casey were 81 and 83. Peter's scores slightly decreased to 78, while Casey's scores slightly increased to 85. At the conclusion of parent mindfulness training, a paired-sample Wilcoxon signed rank result indicated significant reductions in Total Problems scores for the children as a group ($z=1.992$, $n=6$, $p=0.046$).

There was no statistically significant change pre- to post-intervention on subscale measures for each child. For four subscales, anxious/depressed, aggressive behaviour, attention problems and thought problems, there was a trend towards improvement following the intervention for three of the children (Sam, David and Bindy) as indicated by reductions in scores on the four subscales (Fig. 4.5). However, some children showed mixed results. John, Diana's son, demonstrated an increase in anxious/depressed and thought problems, along with a reduction in aggressive behaviour and attention problems. Peter, Mariam's son, demonstrated an increase in aggressive behaviour along with a decrease in anxiety. Casey, Molly's son, showed a slight increase in attention problems and a decrease in anxiety and thought problems. Casey and Peter showed no change in aggressive behaviour and thought problems. In sum, three of the six children show consistent reductions in all four types of challenging behaviour, while the remaining three show mixed results, suggesting some complexity in the effects of the intervention.

The direct and indirect effects of parent mindfulness training are discussed in the following section, along with contextual information gathered from mothers through group discussions and reflective diaries. They are organised according to individual mother–child dyads.

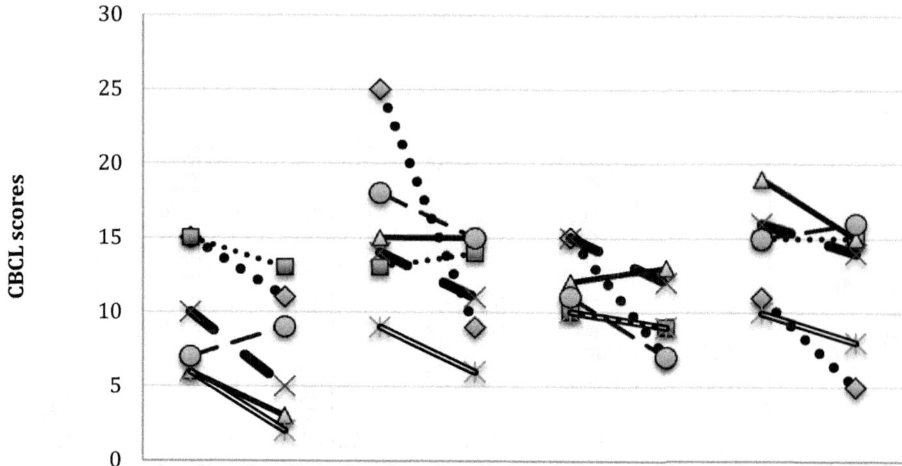

	Anx_Pre	Anx_Post	Agg_Pre	Agg_Post	Att_Pre	Att_Post	TP_Pre	TP_Post
Sam	15	11	25	9	15	7	11	5
Peter	15	13	13	14	10	9	15	15
Casey	6	3	15	15	12	13	19	15
David	10	5	14	11	15	12	16	14
Bindy	6	2	9	6	10	9	10	8
John	7	9	18	15	11	7	15	16

Fig. 4.5 Indirect effects of the parent mindfulness training on children

4.4.3 Effects on Individual Mother–Child Dyads

4.4.3.1 Vicky–Sam

Prior to the training, Vicky expressed her concerns about Sam's aggression towards himself (e.g. punching, hitting and speaking about suicide) and others (e.g. teasing others to make himself feel better, ignoring others because of their appearance, punching a car, kicking a trolley and hitting people), which occurred in both public and private spaces. At the end of the mindfulness training for mothers, Vicky and Sam both showed positive changes in all aspects. Vicky demonstrated increased mindfulness and family quality of life, and decreased parenting stress (Fig. 4.6). According to the CBCL, Sam showed a remarkable decrease, from clinical to normal range, on the scale of aggressive behaviour (from 25 to 10), attention problems (from 15 to 7) and thought problems (from 11 to 5). His Total Problems score was also reduced from 101 to 54.

To understand the improvements reported for Vicky and Sam, we must consider a number of aspects that may have influenced these results. Around the time she participated in this study, Vicky transferred Sam to home education because of his severe anxiety and aggressive behaviour at school. The combination of mindfulness training for Vicky and home schooling for Sam could have influenced both of them. Studying at home may have allowed Sam to manage his stress and anxiety better

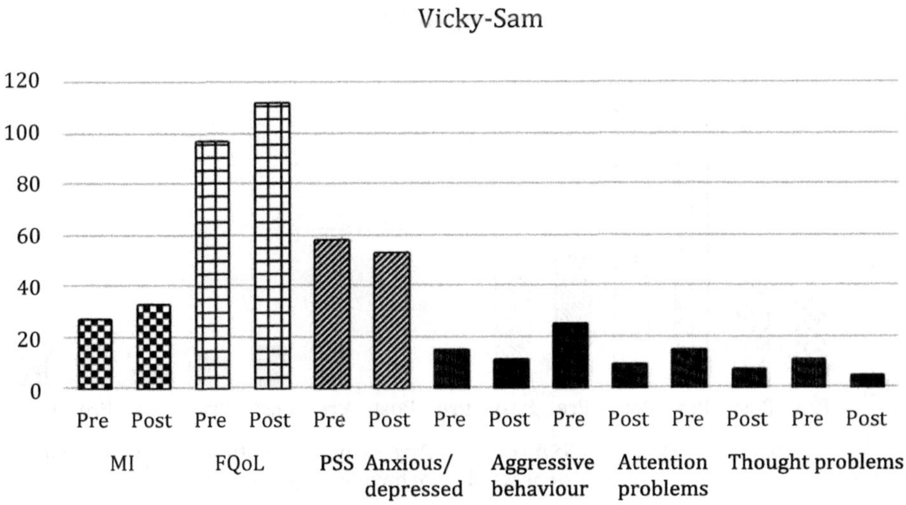

Fig. 4.6 Mindfulness, quality of family life and parental stress of Vicky and challenging behaviour of Sam

than studying at school, and this in turn could have positively influenced Vicky's psychological state.

Taking on the dual responsibility as mother and teacher, however, did not appear to be easy for Vicky. Practising mindfulness seemed to increase her sensitivity to her inner and outer experience. Towards the end of the training, Vicky was shopping with her family when suddenly everything became too much for her, and she broke into screaming and crying. During this crisis, Vicky applied mindfulness to allow her to complete her shopping, and at home continued her practice by mindfully stroking her cat. She saw this event as a significant wake-up call, and after restoring her sense of inner balance she was able to have a calm and honest conversation with her husband about her problems. She wrote, "by being mindful, I had stopped all that negativity in my mind that usually drags me deeper". After her training Vicky wrote about her new sense of calmness when she was mindful of her disturbed feelings and her need to take time out for herself. It appears that mindfulness practice may have helped Vicky relate to her difficulties more skilfully, and the time Vicky and Sam spent together in home schooling could have made him more sensitive to any changes that occurred within her.

4.4.3.2 Diana–John

At the end of training Diana, like Vicky, showed improvement in all three areas of mindfulness, family quality of life and parental stress. She had the largest decrease in parenting stress and the second largest increase in mindfulness (Fig. 4.7). Diana practised mindfulness meditation on a daily basis and kept her reflective journal

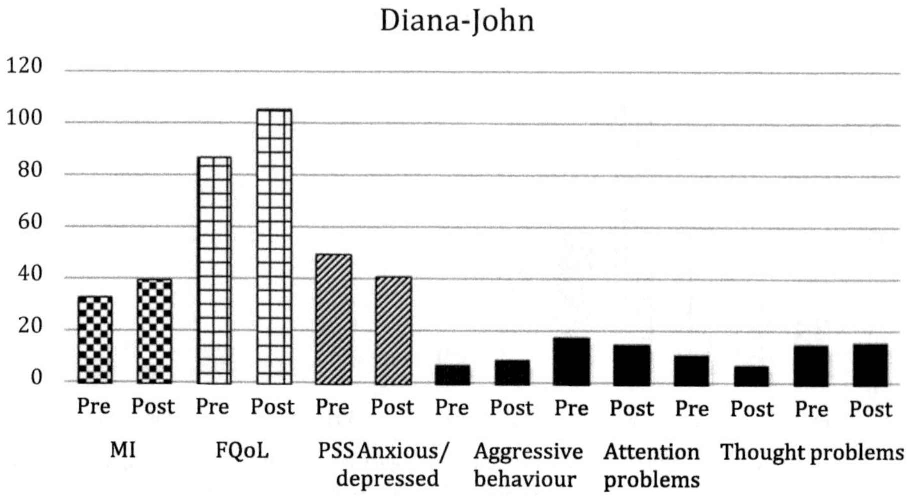

Fig. 4.7 Mindfulness, quality of family life and parental stress of Diana and challenging behaviour of John

diligently. She recognised the importance of incorporating mindfulness practice into everyday life, no matter how briefly. She wrote in her diary that stopping to attend to her breath for 2–4 minutes and focusing on one task at a time reduced her level of stress remarkably. Diana also explicitly applied mindfulness to her parenting practice, which influenced her parenting style. At one training session she said that now when she was with her children she was really paying attention to each one, and she saw they were happier as a result.

Her son, John (CA: 8 years), was the youngest child participant. He was diagnosed with Asperger's syndrome and joined this programme on the strong recommendation of his paediatrician. John attended a mainstream school with support from a paraprofessional for 3 hours per week. Diana's main concern was his non-compliant behaviour, along with his reactions to the perception of being different to his peers. He told Diana that he was "a little bit crazy", although it was not known whether he thought this himself or was repeating what others told him.

At the end of mindfulness training for mothers, mixed results were reported for John. The CBCL completed by Diana showed an increase in anxiety/depression from 7 (normal range) to 9 (borderline clinical range) and thought problems from 15 to 16 (both within clinical range), along with a reduction in aggressive behaviour from 18 (clinical range) to 15 (borderline clinical range) and attention problems from 11 (borderline clinical range) to 7 (normal range). Although the degree of reductions in aggression and attention problems was greater than the increases in anxiety/depression and thought problems, these mixed results suggest that the indirect effects of mindfulness training for children with ASD and challenging behaviour can differ considerably between individuals.

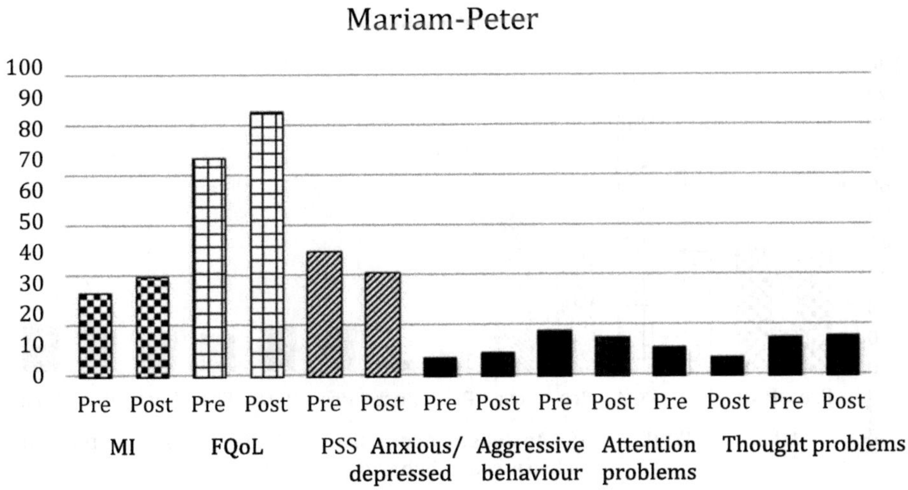

Fig. 4.8 Mindfulness, quality of family life and parental stress of Mariam and challenging behaviour of Peter

4.4.3.3 Mariam–Peter

Mariam–Peter demonstrated mixed results (Fig. 4.8). While Mariam showed the largest improvement in mindfulness, from 30.6 to 41, accompanied by a slight decrease in parenting stress from 60 to 58, her family quality of life declined from 95 to 87. Prior to the training her parenting stress was the highest among the six mothers, but she also reported a high level of family quality of life. At the end of the parent training Peter, Mariam's son, demonstrated an increase in aggressive behaviour from 13 to 14 (both within borderline clinical range), but a decrease in anxiety from 15 to 13 (both within clinical range), and in attention problems from 10 to 9 (both within borderline clinical range).

Mariam reported that she was waking up during the night on fewer occasions, and her mind was calmer. She attributed these changes to her meditation practice. Mariam's relationship to her practice matured over time. She realised that the more she practised being present with her experience, the easier and more interesting her practice became. She wrote in her diary that while her mindfulness practice began as homework she had to complete for the project, over time it turned into an essential means for managing her stress. These reports, gathered from her reflective diary and group discussions, are consistent with her increased mindfulness scores and decreased parental stress level. This increased mindfulness, however, was accompanied by decreased family quality of life.

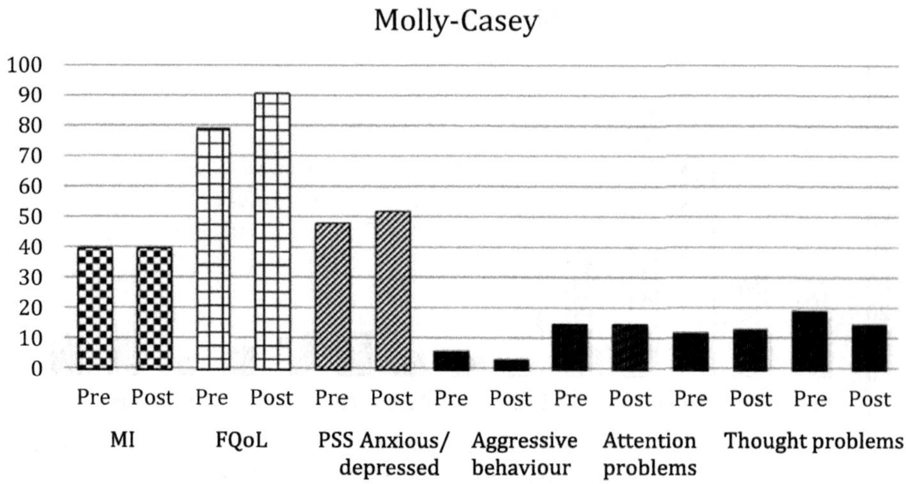

Fig. 4.9 Mindfulness, quality of family life and parental stress of Molly and challenging behaviour of Casey

4.4.3.4 Molly–Casey

Molly and Casey both demonstrated mixed results in the effects of parent mindfulness training (Fig. 4.9). Molly experienced increased family quality of life, from 79 before the training to 91 after the training. This change, however, was accompanied by increased parental stress from 48 to 52 along with an unchanged level of mindfulness. Molly's son, Casey, showed decreased anxiety, from 6 to 3 (both within normal range), and thought problems, from 19 to 15 (both within clinical range), while in attention problems he showed a slight increase, from 12 (borderline clinical range) to 13 (clinical range). His aggressive behaviour remained unchanged at 15 (borderline clinical range).

According to Molly, Casey's challenging behaviour is characterised by verbal and physical aggression. Molly, however, was most concerned by her perception of his disengagement from peers and frequent distractions when learning. This concern appeared to reflect Molly's additional responsibility as his home schooling teacher and her difficulties in engaging him in learning, and may have influenced her parental stress.

Molly was sincerely committed to mindfulness practice. While participating in this study she made her own meditation stool and she practised formal sitting meditation as frequently as possible. She was often very detailed in her descriptions of her meditative experience in her reflective diary and group discussions. In her diary she wrote of her discovery of the potency of mindfulness in everyday activities, with the realisation that setting aside a special time to meditate was not strictly necessary as she could practice in any situation, even in the shower. She also realised that when she was more relaxed and contented with herself she was also more relaxed and contented with her children, including Casey. Taken together, these

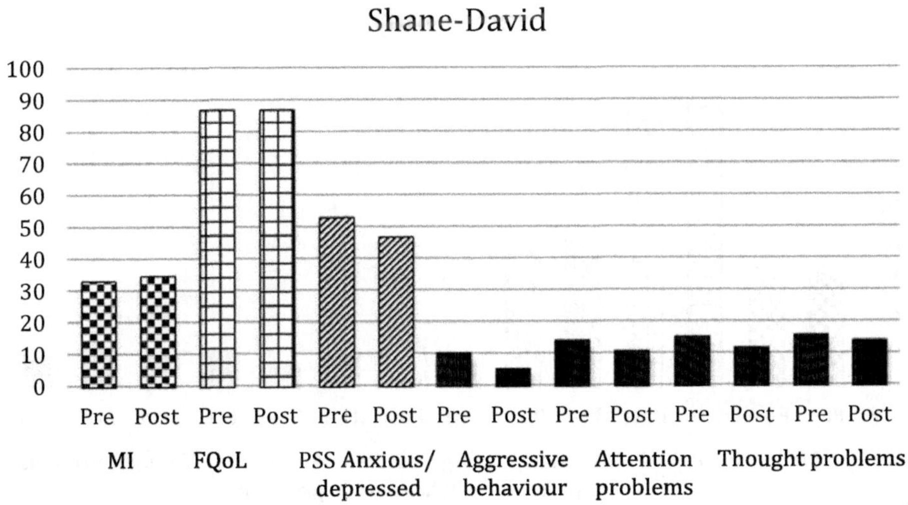

Fig. 4.10 Mindfulness, quality of family life and parental stress of Shane and challenging behaviour of David

experiences indicate that Molly may have become more sensitive to all the changes of her inner states, including both pleasant (e.g. family quality of life) and painful (e.g. parenting stress), and this may account for her mixed results.

4.4.3.5 Shane–David

Shane (CA: 48 years) was the oldest mother participant and her son, David (CA: 15 years), was the oldest child participant in this study. They both showed consistently positive changes at the end of the mindfulness training for mothers (Fig. 4.10). Shane's mindfulness increased from 33 to 35 and her parental stress decreased from 53 to 47, while her family quality of life remained the same at 87. David's CBCL indicated a reduction in anxiety from 10 (clinical range) to 5 (normal range), in aggression from 14 (borderline clinical range) to 11 (normal range), in attention from 15 (clinical range) to 12 (borderline clinical range), and in thought problems from 16 to 14 (both within clinical range).

Shane was motivated to join this project because of the growing tension, stress and anger among her family members. In the beginning, she frequently experienced bodily discomfort and pain in her meditation, along with distractions caused by random and restless thoughts. As the training progressed she began to appreciate the relaxing and peaceful nature of meditation, although she continued to struggle with unwanted thoughts. In week 7 Shane reported "a humungous difference" in her household. She reported that the number of "blow-outs" that occurred in her family had reduced from about five times a week before the project to once or twice a week. Shane said, "I guess that is in me, maybe in how I handle it. I don't know, but it's a huge difference".

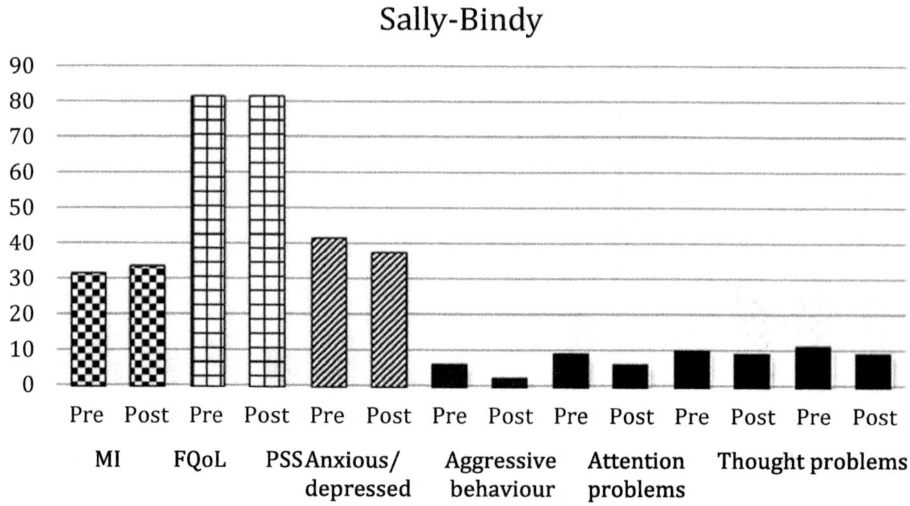

Fig. 4.11 Mindfulness, quality of family life and parental stress of Sally and challenging behaviour of Bindy

At the end of the parental mindfulness training David showed reductions in all four areas of challenging behaviour, with two of them reduced to normal range. These include aggressive behaviour, perceived by Shane as his most worrying problem, along with a reluctance to communicate with his family. David is currently in a mainstream secondary school and has recently been diagnosed with Asperger's syndrome. While it is impossible to establish a simple causal relationship between Shane's mindfulness practice and David's improved behaviour, it is possible that the changes in Shane may have created a more relaxed family environment that facilitated changes in David.

4.4.3.6 Sally–Bindy

At the end of the parent training period both Sally and Bindy demonstrated positive changes in all measured aspects (Fig. 4.11). Sally showed slightly increased mindfulness from 32 to 34 and reduced parental stress from 42 to 38, along with an unchanged family quality of life at 82. For Bindy, anxiety decreased from 6 to 2 (both within normal range), aggressive behaviour from 9 to 6 (both within normal range), attention problems from 10 to 9 (both within borderline clinical range) and thought problems from 11 to 9 (both within clinical range).

Although the overall results for both Sally and Bindy were relatively positive, it was clear that Sally struggled with maintaining a regular mindfulness practice and maintaining her reflective diary during the training period. She demonstrated a cycle of intending to practise mindfulness, having difficulty in actually practising it, experiencing frustration and guilt from not meeting her own expectations, culminating in anger. More than anything else, Sally's motivation to participate in this study was her desire to address her own anger, which was something she constantly struggled with. Although it was explained to her that mindfulness is a long-term solution that required long-term practice, she often spoke of her hope that her problems could be resolved quickly.

Sally was most concerned about her daughter's tendency to complain when there was any change in her routine, her habit to try to please people by answering their questions impulsively, and her "extremely" aggressive behaviour of hitting, biting and kicking. Yet Sally's CBCL assessment prior to the programme indicated that Bindy's aggressive behaviour and anxiety were relatively low, since they were within the normal range. At the end of the training they were even lower. According to Sally, Bindy tended to exhibit challenging behaviour in response to Sally's parenting style. Sally said, "What I see more of lately, because I don't push to melt-down point anymore. I used to push to melt-down point and then she would bite or whatever". It is possible that Bindy's challenging behaviour declined because of Sally's increasing sensitivity to the impact of her own actions on her daughter.

4.5 Conclusion

In this chapter we have presented the parent training intervention for six mothers of children with ASD and challenging behaviours. We have provided the theoretical background for the development of a new mindfulness programme, called Inclusive Mindfulness. From there, we described how the second author developed an approach to teaching mindfulness that would be sufficiently flexible to accommodate the unique requirements of this intervention, that of training mothers to become both mindfulness practitioners themselves and the mindfulness teachers of their own children. We then outlined the eight-week programme for mothers as taught by the two authors, showing the themes and practices that were developed during that period. Finally, we described the participants in terms of mother–child dyads and outlined the results for each dyad as measured at the end of the parent training intervention. In the next chapter, we will present the parent-mediated child mindfulness training and its results.

References

Achenbach, T. M., & Rescorla, L. A. (2001). *Manual for the ASEBA school-age forms & profiles*. Burlington: University of Vermont, Research Center for Children, Youth, & Families.

Anālayo. (2006). *Satipatthana: The direct path to realization*. Birmingham: Windhorse Publications.

Berry, J. D., & Jones, W. H. (1995). The parental stress scale: Initial psychometric evidence. *Journal of Social and Personal Relationships, 12,* 463–472.

Bodhi, B. (1994). *The noble eightfold path: Way to the end of suffering* (2nd ed.). Kandy: Buddhist Publication Society.

Bodhi, B. (Ed.). (2000). *Abhidhammattha sangaha. A comprehensive manual of abhidhamma.* Seattle: BPS Pariyatti

Bodhi, B. (2005). *In the Buddha's words. An anthology of discourses from the Pāli canon.* Boston: Wisdom Publications.

Bodhi, B. (2012). *The numerical discourses of the Buddha: A translation of the Anguttara Nikaya.* Boston: Wisdom Publications.

Braun, V., & Clarke, V. (2006). Using thematic analysis in psychology. *Qualitative Research in Psychology, 3,* 77–101.

Dennett, D. C. (1991). *Consciousness explained.* Boston: Little, Brown & Company.

Gethin, R. (1998). *The foundations of Buddhism.* Oxford: Oxford University Press.

Gethin, R. (2001). *The Buddhist path to awakening: A study of the bodhi-pakkhiyā-dhammā.* Oxford: Oneworld Publications.

Gowans, C. W. (2003). *Philosophy of the Buddha.* London: Routledge.

Gunaratana, H. (1985). *The path of serenity and insight.* Delhi: Motilal Banarsidass Publishers.

Higgins, W. (2012). The coming of secular Buddhism: A synoptic view. *Journal of Global Buddhism, 13,* 109–126.

Hoffman, L., Marquis, J. G., Poston, D. J., Summers, J. A., & Turnbull, A. (2006). Assessing family outcomes: Psychometric evaluation of the family quality of life scale. *Journal of Marriage and Family, 68,* 1069–1083.

Hwang, Y. S., & Kearney, P. (2013). A systematic review of mindfulness intervention for individuals with developmental disabilities: Long-term practice and long lasting effects. *Research in Developmental Disabilities, 34,* 314–326.

Jordt, I. (2007). *Burma's mass lay meditation movement: Buddhism and the cultural construction of power.* Athens: Ohio University Press.

Kabat-Zinn, J. (2003). Mindfulness-based interventions in context: Past, present, and future. *Clinical Psychology: Science and Practice, 10,* 144–156.

Kalupahana, D. J. (1969). A Buddhist tract on empiricism. *Philosophy East and West, 19*(1), 65–67.

Kalupahana, D. J. (1988). *Dhamma (1) Encyclopaedia of Buddhism* (Vol. 4 (Fascicle 3), pp. 438–453). Ceylon: Government of Ceylon.

Kalupahana, D. J. (1992). *A history of Buddhist philosophy. continuities & discontinuities.* Honolulu: University of Hawaii Press.

Karunadasa, Y. (1996). *The dhamma theory. Philosophical cornerstone of the Abhidhamma.* Kandy: Buddhist Publication Society.

Kuan, T.-f. (2008). *Mindfulness in early Buddhism: New approaches through psychology and textual analysis of Pali, Chinese and Sanskrit sources.* London: Routledge.

Maharaj, S. N. (1998). *I am that. Talks with Sri Nisargadatta Maharaj* (M. Frydman, Trans.). Durham: Acorn Press.

Mahasi. (1971). *Practical insight meditation. Basic and progressive stages.* Kandy: Buddhist Publication Society.

McCown, D., Reibel, D., & Micozzi, M. S. (2011). *Teaching mindfulness: A practical guide for clinicians and educators.* New York: Springer.

McMahan, D. L. (2008). *The making of Buddhist modernism.* Oxford: Oxford University Press.

Nyanatiloka. (1980). *Buddhist dictionary. Manual of Buddhist terms and doctrines* (4th ed.). Kandy: Buddhist Publication Society.

Oord, S. v. d., Bögels, S., & Peijnenburg, D. (2012). The effectiveness of mindfulness training for children with ADHD and mindful parenting for their parents. *Journal of Child Family Studies, 21,* 139–147.

Pandita, S. U. (1993). *In this very life: The liberation teachings of the Buddha* (2nd ed.). Boston: Wisdom Publications.

Rhys Davids, T. W., & Stede, W. (Eds.). (1999). The Pali Text Society's Pali-English dictionary. Oxford: The Pali Text Society.

Segal, Z. V., Williams, J. M. G., & Teasdale, J. D. (2002). *Mindfulness-based cognitive therapy for depression: A new approach to preventing relapse*. New York: Guilford.

Smith, S. W., Daunic, A. P., & Taylor, G. G. (2007). Treatment fidelity in applied educational research: Expanding the adoption and application of measures to ensure evidence-based practice. *Education and Treatment of Children, 30*(4), 121–134.

Thanissaro. (1996). *The wings to awakening. An anthology from the Pali Canon*. Massachusetts: Dhamma Dana Publications.

Thera, N. (1969). *The heart of Buddhist meditation*. London: Rider & Company.

Thera, Ñ. (1987). *Clearing the path: Writings of Ñāṇavīra Thera (1960–1965)*. Colombo: Path Press.

Walach, H., Buchheld, N., Buttenmuller, V., Kleinknecht, N., & Schmidt, S. (2006). Measuring mindfulness-the Freiburg Mindfulness Inventory (FMI). *Personality and Individual Differences, 40,* 1543–1555.

Warder, A. K. (1980). *Indian Buddhism* (2nd ed.). Delhi: Motilal Banarsidass.

Chapter 5
Study Two: Mindfulness Intervention for Children

This chapter presents the theoretical framework, development, delivery and effects of the parent-implemented mindfulness intervention for the six children with autism spectrum disorder (ASD) and challenging behaviours (stage 2). The aim of this intervention was to train these children to the point where they could use mindfulness meditation to manage their own problem behaviour. We begin by exploring the contemporary educational theories and practices that constitute the theoretical framework for the intervention, those of universal design for learning (UDL), differentiation, self-determination, video modelling and parent-implemented learning. These were employed to meet the range of individuality that characterises ASD. We then explain how these activities were developed and delivered to the six children.

Individually responsive learning was fundamental to the programme, beginning with in-depth interviews with each child to assist with design of the mindfulness activities. The interviews were supported by a choice of preferred modes of communication that applied the principle of self-determination, and an arts-based research approach. Initial mindfulness activities were developed for the children, based on the range of mental experiences they expressed. They were designed to ground their attention over time using bodily movement, sounds, breathing and mental states and were later enhanced by an additional two activities.

This chapter also presents the intervention process and methods, such as home visits, online meetings and video modelling, along with issues that arose during delivery including compatibility between teacher and learner, the variety of responses from the children to the mindfulness training, and intervention fidelity. Finally, we monitored any possible differences in the behaviours of these children at the conclusion of their parent-implemented mindfulness intervention, and any intervention effects for the mothers who taught them. The ultimate goal of stages 1 and 2 together is to strengthen and empower the family as a unit (Table 5.1).

Y.-S. Hwang, P. Kearney, *A Mindfulness Intervention for Children with Autism Spectrum Disorder*, Mindfulness in Behavioral Health,
DOI 10.1007/978-3-319-18962-8_5

Table 5.1 Aims and effects of stage 1 and 2 interventions

	Aim 1	Aim 2	Direct effects	Indirect effects
Stage 1: Mindfulness intervention for mothers	Use mindfulness to help mothers in their own lives	Train mothers to become mindfulness teachers for their own child	Intervention effects for mothers	Intervention effects for children
Stage 2: Mindfulness intervention for children	Use mindfulness to address children's challenging behaviours		Intervention effects for children	Intervention effects for mothers

5.1 Theoretical Framework of the Inclusive Mindfulness (IM) Programme for Children

5.1.1 Universal Design for Learning and Differentiation

Autism spectrum disorder (ASD) has two primary diagnostic markers, impairments in social communication and social interaction, and restricted repetitive patterns of behaviour (American Psychiatric Association, 2013). ASD is often characterised by heterogeneity in the width and depth of difficulties in social, communicative and/or behavioural functions (Happé, Ronald, & Plomin, 2006), resulting in a wide range of individually different learning requirements. This heterogeneity creates difficulties for educators and professionals in providing individually responsive learning opportunities (Hwang, Klieve, Kearney, & Saggers, 2013). We adopted universal design for learning (UDL) and differentiation to address the learning preferences and styles of these six children with ASD.

UDL is an inclusive approach to curriculum development that enhances access to learning for diverse learners. UDL provides a set of educational principles that guide the adjustment of instructional goals, methods, materials and assessments for individual needs (CAST, 2013). They apply flexibility and multiplicity to the presentation of information and concepts, the expression or performance of what is learned, and the engagement of learners (Rose & Meyer, 2002).

A wide range of studies have demonstrated the benefits of using UDL for enhancing learning outcomes. For example, Coyne, Pisha, Dalton, Zeph and Smith (2010) examined and reported greater gains in the reading comprehension of students with intellectual disability who received a technology-based UDL literacy instruction compared to those who received literacy instruction designed and delivered without consideration of UDL principles. It is essential to develop an understanding of learner differences to design and deliver the kinds of learning content and processes that enable a variety of learners to progress in the curriculum (Meo, 2008).

Differentiation is an individually focused educational approach within which human differences are viewed as greatly influencing the learning and teaching of a common set of critical content (Tomlinson & Imbeau, 2010). Respect for learner diversity and flexibility is fundamental. Teachers are required to adjust the learning content (i.e. curriculum), processes (i.e. instruction) and products (i.e. assessment) by taking account of individual students' learning readiness, interest and profiles (Lewis & Batts, 2005). As in UDL, the process of differentiating curriculum and instruction begins by developing an understanding of the learners (Udvari-Solner, Villa, & Thousand, 2005), on the basis of which educators do whatever it takes to provide them with opportunities for learning success (Wormeli, 2006).

In summary, the fundamental principle of UDL and differentiation is the provision of responsive education for all learners, achieved through flexible learning and teaching practices tailored by an understanding of the individuality of learners. These principles are already fundamental to mindfulness interventions for people in general. They are, however, even more critical in mindfulness interventions for those with disabilities, such as ASD. The following sections, *5.2 Development of IM Programme* and *5.3 Delivery of IM Programme*, show how the theory and practice of UDL and differentiation guided the process of developing and delivering mindfulness activities for these six children with ASD and challenging behaviour.

5.1.2 Self-Determination

Self-determination is another evidence-based best practice for students with disability. In education, self-determination refers to "the volitional actions that enable one to act as the primary causal agent in one's life and to maintain or improve one's quality of life" (Wehmeyer, 2010, p. 857). It was originally rooted in the intention to empower people with disability and to protect their right to make choices in their own lives (Wehmeyer et al., 2012). Self-determined behaviour includes a range of critical elements, including choice-making skills, decision-making skills, problem-solving skills, self-management and self-regulation skills, self-awareness and self-knowledge (Wehmeyer, 2011). The acquisition and development of these elements takes lifelong practice and needs to begin early in one's life (Wehmeyer et al., 2012).

Research has demonstrated the benefits of training people with disability in self-determination. People with disabilities who are self-determined are more likely than their less self-determined counterparts to achieve positive academic (Lee, Wehmeyer, Palmer, Soukup, & Little, 2008), employment and independent living outcomes (Wehmeyer & Palmer, 2003; Wehmeyer & Schwartz, 1997), along with a better quality of life (Shogren, Lopez, Wehmeyer, Little, & Pressgrove, 2006). Self-directed learning is an additional benefit of training people with disability in self-determination (Wehmeyer et al., 2012), leading to more meaningful involvement in learning. An example of this would be individuals with disability participating in intervention design and setting their own learning plan and goals according to their own interests, abilities and requirements.

Self-determination and mindfulness practice naturally go together. Learning and practising mindfulness is a self-directed and self-managed procedure. The continuous attention required to remember and thus sustain awareness cannot be externally forced. In addition, as discussed in Chap. 3, the proven benefits for individuals with disability of practising mindfulness include increased capacities to manage one's own behavioural and/or psychological issues on the basis of self-awareness. Self-awareness and self-management are integral elements of self-determined behaviour. Consequently, the concept of self-directed learning was a natural fit for the delivery of the Inclusive Mindfulness (IM) programme.

5.1.3 Video Modelling

Video modelling is an evidence-based intervention strategy based on Bandura's social learning theory, within which children are believed to learn essential skills by observing and imitating other people performing them (Bellini & Akullian, 2007). Video modelling entails children watching video demonstrations of targeted skills performed by themselves (i.e. self-modelling) or others (Delano, 2007). It is known to be effective for individuals with ASD in acquiring such essential skills as social communication (Nikopoulos & Keenan, 2007) and functional life activities (Charlop-Christy, Le, & Freeman, 2000).

Attention and motivation are both vital to observational learning, since imitation of a modelled behaviour will not occur if a child does not attend to the model (Bellini & Akullian, 2007). The most successful outcomes of video modelling are expected when direct instruction of targeted skills is paired with practice opportunities that occur in natural contexts (Schreibman & Ingersoll, 2005). *Section 5.3 Delivery of IM programme* details how this approach was implemented when teaching mindfulness activities to the six children with ASD and challenging behaviour.

5.1.4 Parent-Implemented Learning

Parent-implemented learning involves training parents to teach new skills, such as language and communication, to their own child in home or community settings (Kaiser & Hancock, 2003). Parents are often the most constant teachers of their own children, and they possess an accumulation of knowledge regarding their child's development that professionals lack. Parents therefore should be invited to play a central role in their children's intervention programmes to make use of their expertise (Mahoney & Wiggers, 2007). Parent-implemented learning has a range of advantages. Cheaper and less resource-intensive, parent-implemented interventions in naturalistic settings can enhance the generalisation and maintenance of learned skills (Matson, Mahan, & Matson, 2009). More importantly, this approach empowers parents as it enables them to build their own capacity to teach their children effectively (Matson et al., 2009).

Overall, the results of research into parent-implemented learning have been positive. Wong et al. (2013) identified parent-meditated intervention as an evidence-based practice. The results of a review of 456 intervention studies for children, youth and young adults with ASD indicated that parents delivered interventions to their children with ASD effectively, generating positive social, communicational, academic and/or behavioural outcomes, especially for toddlers (0–2 years) to primary school-aged learners (6–11 years). A recent Cochrane review provided further data. Oono, Honey and McConachie (2013) reviewed 17 randomised controlled studies to investigate the effectiveness of parent-implemented early interventions for children with ASD and their parents and found evidence to support previous findings of improved interactions between parents and their children.

Like other intervention practices, parent-implemented learning is not without its difficulties. Not every parent is ready and willing to learn the strategies necessary to teach their child (Kaiser & Hancock, 2003). Elevated stress has been frequently reported for parents of a child with ASD (e.g. Eisenhower, Baker, & Blacher, 2005; Harper, Dyches, Harper, Roper, & South, 2013; Silva & Schalock, 2012) and taking up a teaching role may exacerbate their existing stress. This caution was acknowledged in the Cochrane review results, which suggested the need for practitioners of parent-implemented interventions to carefully monitor parent stress levels (Oono et al., 2013). It is therefore important to consider not only parents' readiness to learn new skills for their children's development, but also their time and energy (Kaiser & Hancock, 2003).

While these problems have the potential to affect the psychological wellbeing of parent teachers, parent-implemented learning can be valuable, and especially for parents who struggle with a lack of professional support. As children with ASD grow older and enter into their teen years, the availability of professional support services for their family declines (Keller & Honig, 2004; White & Hastings, 2004). Equipping parents with new skills important for their children with ASD through well-designed parent-implemented learning can support their families, for example by improving the quality of interactions between parents and their children with ASD (Oono et al., 2013). Section 5.3 *Delivery of IM programme* details how this approach was put into practice when teaching mindfulness activities to the six children with ASD and challenging behaviour.

5.2 Development of IM Programme

5.2.1 Frameworks for Individual Semi-structured Interviews

Individual semi-structured interviews were conducted with the six children with ASD and challenging behaviour to explore their learning readiness and any requirements they might have for the mindfulness intervention. Remembering that learners are the foundation for responsive education (e.g. Meo, 2008; Tomlinson & Imbeau, 2010; Udvari-Solner et al., 2005), gaining descriptive data from qualitative research methods, such as interviews, leads to a deeper understanding of individuals with disability and their heterogeneous learning requirements (Brantlinger, Jimenez, Klingner, Pugach, & Richardson, 2005). This is the first step in an evidence-based process for individuals with ASD and ID and functions as a tool for identifying individual attitudes, values and opinions (West, McCollow, Gumbarger, Kidwell, & Cote, 2013).

ASD is characterised by social communication difficulties (American Psychiatric Association, 2013). People with ASD often find it difficult to communicate and comprehend abstract concepts, such as thoughts and feelings (Spek, van Ham, & Nyklicek, 2013). They tend to experience heightened anxiety when they communicate with people who are strange to them (Nazeer, 2006), and this can add extra hardship to their already existing communication difficulties when they participate in interviews. To help overcome these difficulties, we utilised principles of self-determination by providing the children with a choice of preferred communication mode, whether speaking, writing or typing, during their interview sessions. We also used drawings, either produced by the children or selected from ASD literature (i.e. Howlin, Baron-Cohen, & Hadwin, 1999), to assist conversations about abstract concepts such as thoughts and feelings. For example, a self-produced portrait was used to explore the children's feelings by pointing at the portrait and asking, "How do you feel in this drawing?" More detailed information on the use of similar methods in the course of qualitative research into the affective experiences of students with ASD and cognitive difficulties can be found elsewhere (Hwang, 2014).

We minimised the possibility of provoking anxiety during interviews in the following ways. Prior to the interviews, mothers had been asked to bring items that had a calming effect on their child in case they became agitated during the interview. The mothers were also asked to tell their child in advance of the details of the interview arrangements, including times, venue (i.e. quiet room at the university the first author was affiliated with) and interviewer (i.e. the first author), so they could have clear expectations regarding the encounter. At the beginning of the initial interview, the first author used an animation character she had created as an icebreaker. This character introduced the purpose of the interview to the children and informed them of their right to request a break or quit the interviews, and could choose whether they wanted their mother to be present or absent during the interview.

The aim of the individual interviews was to explore anything that could help make the mindfulness activities under development responsive to the individuality of each child. The systematic review of mindfulness intervention studies for individuals with developmental disabilities, including ASD, identified breathing, bodily sensations and mental states as the objects of experience most commonly used as foundations for the grounding of attention over time (Hwang & Kearney, 2013). Acknowledging this review result, the interviews focused on revealing the degree of the children's capacity to be aware of their own physical and mental experience. Table 5.2 presents examples of interview questions. The questions were organised in such a way for the children to begin with the less complex and then move on to the more complex. They were therefore structured from closed-ended to open-ended and from concrete to abstract.

Table 5.2 Examples of interview questions

Interview topic	Spoken format	Written format (self-completion by handwriting or typing)
Love	Who/what do you love?	I love ()
Feelings	When do you feel happy?	I feel happy when ()
	What do you do when you are angry?	When I am angry I ()
	How does your mum feel when you are sick?	When I am sick, my mum feels ()
Thoughts	What do you often think about?	I often think about ()
Senses	Is there any sound you would like to hear?	I like to hear ()
	Is there any flavour you don't like?	I don't like to taste ()

5.2.2 *Results of Individual Semi-structured Interviews*

The interview data were transcribed verbatim and analysed using thematic analysis (Braun & Clarke, 2006). The analysis results indicated that the majority of children were aware of their own physical and mental experiences. "Happy" was the most frequently mentioned state. However, when their experiences are classified into the categories of pleasant (indicating all forms of pleasure and happiness) and unpleasant (indicating all forms of pain and distress), then the range of vocabulary they employed for pleasant states was quite limited compared with the range they used for unpleasant states. Their expressions of pleasant states were limited to "happy" and "good", while their expressions of unpleasant states included "angry", "annoyed", "disappointed", "grumpy", "irritated", "scared" and "sad". Overall, the children expressed unpleasant experiences more frequently than pleasant ones, for example when they described occasions in which they physically attacked others or were physically attacked by others. We explore the children's understanding of their physical and mental experience in the following sections.

John was 8 years old and had been diagnosed with Asperger's and PDD-NOS. The youngest of the six child participants, John said he was "very proud of himself" for coming to a university for an interview at such a young age. He was fluent in identifying his physical and mental experience, and the links between the two. He explained that when he was scared, he felt "achy in the throat", and when he was angry, he felt "a bit hot" in his tummy. When he was really angry, he felt "like punching people". He said, "I tried to keep it in. Sometimes I can't keep it in. I just punch people". He cries after punching people because he feels "very sorry" and "sad". He also said that crying made him feel a bit better. He expressed his affection for his family, especially for his mother. He knew she did not want him to hurt other children, and he felt sad when she was saddened by his behaviour.

Sam was 10 years old and had been diagnosed with Asperger's and HFA. Sam wanted to become an architect who designs houses, and he portrayed himself as "not as special as other people, just the same". He was fluent in identifying his own physical and mental experiences and demonstrated a capacity to remember the past in great detail. He appeared to be more sensitive to painful physical and mental states than pleasant ones. In particular, he discussed his experiences of hurting others and himself feeling hurt, sad, worried and trapped. He said that when he was seven, he used to hit people and kick the dog, calling this "horrible" behaviour and at one point muttering, "Lucky I am not seven". In response to the question how he knew he was sad, he talked about "feeling worried in the stomach" and his need to "vomit to get rid of the trapped feeling in the stomach". This indicates Sam was not only able to identify both his physical and mental experience, but he could also identify the links between them.

Casey was 10 years old and had been diagnosed with PDD-NOS. Casey was intrigued by sounds. During the interviews, he often made farting noises, using his lips and armpits. Although he thought making a fart sound was funny, he knew it could irritate people, especially his little brother. Casey found his little brother annoying and said, "I often beat him in a fight. I could tease him and beat him in a fight". Casey was sensitive to his experience of pain, frequently discussing his physical pain. He typed that he was angry when he got hurt, and when asked how he knew he was hurt, he replied, "The nerves, they feel pain and send a message to the brain". Casey expressed his care for his mother by typing that when his mother is happy he feels happy, and when she is sad he feels sad.

Peter was 12 years old and had been diagnosed with HFA, mild intellectual impairment, Tourette's and acute anxiety. Peter was able to identify both his physical and his mental experience. He said people chatting with him made him feel happy, while people pushing, hitting or kicking him at school made him feel sad. He only occasionally reported incidents of physical aggression to his teacher, and was hesitant to do so because he was worried about his friends. Peter said, "It's just because, when I feel like talking and something really bad happens to my friend, I don't talk about it".

Upon further questioning, it became apparent that Peter had difficulty in identifying whether any given incident of physical aggression really was aggression or was just play. He spoke about playing tag, his favourite game, with his classmates. "Well, when Jonathan tags me, he does this, which means he isn't hitting me, he's tagging me. But he doesn't say tag because I understand that he tagged me". He then added, "They don't really hit me when I'm playing tag very often". Another indication of Peter's difficulty in interpreting his social world came from his misunderstanding of the facial expressions of passing pedestrians. When he saw people at school frowning, he used to think they were frowning at him because they were annoyed with him, so he would become annoyed in return. This irritation contributed to his problem behaviour at school. He said, "I know it's not at me, they're concentrating".

Bindy was 12 years old and had been diagnosed with ASD. Bindy said she liked to watch Teletubbies and drink hot water, but named orange juice, chicken nuggets and McDonalds as things she both liked and disliked. She often communicated by repeating a part of the question and then saying what other people would have told her in a given situation. For example, when she was given a hot drink she asked for she said, “It could hurt you”. In self-completion statements, she often provided the same answer to two contrasting questions. For example, she typed “flower” to complete “I don’t like to smell ()” and “I like to smell ()”, and “eat” to complete “I don’t like to taste ()” and “I like to taste ()”. She typed that she felt happy when she was with her friend and typed her own name as that of her friend. She demonstrated her bodily awareness by pointing, when instructed, to her face, arms, stomach, hand and foot as portrayed on her self-portrait. She also said she was a boy.

David was 15 years old and had been diagnosed with ASD. David liked music and wanted to build his career on it. He was greatly interested in online games and was aware of his difficulty in making social connections with people. He often compared himself with others to emphasise that he was not different, adding the expression “like everybody” when he spoke about himself. He named anger as the feeling he experienced most frequently, for example when he lost a game such as Minecraft. He used to break things and knock them over when he was angry. He described his strong anger as, “I might take rage on myself or something. I don’t know, something like that”. He had recently asked his mother to get a punching bag for him, thinking, “This could do wonders”. He said, “I don’t want to throw my phone around the room. I don’t want things to break cause they used to. Like if I got really angry, um, I’d probably snap pencils, break something I might really love, as a kid of course, and, uh, after getting angry I’d get really upset because I just lost something that was mine, something like that”. Although David still found barking dogs and little children annoying, he said he was not as angry as he used to be.

Guided by the concepts of UDL, differentiation and self-determination, the individual interviews were conducted to develop an understanding of the individuality of the children with ASD and challenging behaviour to guide the development of mindfulness activities that would be responsive to their particular situations. Analysis of the interview data highlighted the children’s awareness of their own physical and mental experience. We developed mindfulness activities based on bodily movement awareness to accommodate sensitivity to physical experience, and mindfulness activities based on psychological awareness to accommodate sensitivity to the painful quality of negative thinking. The next section details the development of these mindfulness activities.

5.2.3 Development of Mindfulness Activities

5.2.3.1 Basic Principles

The challenge in this project was to develop mindfulness activities that would be suitable for individuals with ASD and challenging behaviour whose ages ranged from 8 to 15. We could not assume beforehand that any particular mindfulness exercise would be suitable for all, or even any, of them. Rather, we had to experiment with provisional exercises and then, in partnership with their mothers, explore their suitability.

According to the tradition, mindfulness is stimulated by a clear perception (Bodhi, 2000). A mindfulness activity suitable for this population would be one based on a perception that was clear to the child practitioner and that could hold his or her attention over time. We therefore developed four basic mindfulness activities focused on the movement of the body itself and one activity of listening to sounds (Appendix 1). All the exercises were brief, and each ended with the statement, "Smile, and thank yourself".

Five videos were developed, each featuring one of the researchers demonstrating the activity and the other providing a guiding soundtrack. The videos ranged in length from three and a half minutes to almost eight minutes. They were inserted into an app and made available to the child practitioners on their iPads.

5.2.3.2 Five Activities

Cat walking (video = 6.5 min): This is an exercise in slow, careful and rhythmic walking, "like a cat". It is designed to facilitate continuous attention to the body by focusing on movement. The activity appeals to the imagination, as the practitioner imagines oneself as a cat silently stalking a mouse. This gives the activity the quality of a game, and we felt it important to convey a sense of playfulness in this exercise. While demonstrated in the video as a very slow movement, it can be done at any speed. Regardless of speed, it is important that the practitioner has a sense of rhythm in its performance, because rhythm helps the continuity of attention and therefore of mindfulness. We added a recitation of "front-heel-slide" to the walking instructions, to convey the emphasis in this exercise of walking on the ball of the foot rather than the heel and of gliding the weight of the body forward.

Figure 8 (video = 6 min): This activity begins with grounding oneself in the standing posture and making a figure eight with one arm, the movement centred on a relaxed wrist. The eight becomes first bigger, and then smaller. This exercise is simple and employs a relaxed and repetitive movement that, like walking, helps hold attention. It ends with the hands resting on the practitioner's abdomen. After the movement of the arm the practitioner is invited to remain standing for a minute or two and continue to feel movement, here the more subtle movements within the abdomen associated with breathing. This activity therefore follows a trajectory from a comparatively gross object of awareness—the waving of the arm—to a subtle one—the breathing sensed in the abdomen.

Waving (video = 3.24 min): A variation of Fig. 8, this also is a standing exercise. It entails slowly waving both arms up and down in front, leading from the wrists. The waves begin at shoulder height and gradually become smaller. They end with the hands resting on the practitioner's abdomen, as in Fig. 8. The practitioner is invited to remain standing for a minute or two, feeling the movements of the breathing within the abdomen. Again, the awareness of the practitioner moves from comparatively gross to subtle.

Lion lying (video = 7.56 min): This activity invites an experience of stillness. The practitioner lies on his back with hands resting on the belly. The emphasis in this activity is relaxation. The practitioner is invited to tune into the movements of the breathing and progressively relax the whole body, allowing him to sink into the sense of hardness and solidity provided by the ground beneath. As the body relaxes the breathing becomes apparent through the movements of the chest and abdomen and the sensations of the hands resting upon the body, as they rise and fall in time with the breathing.

Sound (video = 5.09 min): This activity involves mindfulness of sound. In the video it is demonstrated as a sitting exercise, although it can also be done standing or lying down. The practitioner is invited to relax and tune into breathing and is then asked to listen to whatever she can hear. Then a bell is struck, and the practitioner is asked to relax and listen to the sound without resistance; to allow it to "go straight through". Another sound is struck, and as its volume gradually decreases the practitioner is asked to recognise the moment the sound ceases. After doing this several times—on the video, it is demonstrated twice—the practitioner is invited to listen to any sound available.

5.2.3.3 An Additional Three Activities

Mindfulness of Mind The five activities above constituted the beginning point of the intervention for the child practitioners. As the intervention proceeded, adjustments were made according to the responses of particular child practitioners. The transcripts for these additional mindfulness activities are found in Appendix 2. One line of development was a movement from mindfulness of body to mindfulness of mind.

For example, Sam had acute anxiety and appeared to be preoccupied by the scenarios created by his thinking. He also had a background in cognitive behaviour therapy, where he had been trained to become sensitive to his own thinking. One principle of mindfulness practice is that any experience can become an object of mindfulness, including one's obstacles and distractions (e.g. Mahasi, 1971). Following this principle, we developed Clouds and Sky, an exercise in which thinking itself is the object of mindfulness.

Once the posture is established and attention directed to breathing, the practitioner is guided into visualising his mind as the open sky. Thoughts are imagined as being like clouds moving through the emptiness of the sky. These clouds may be bright or dark, interesting or boring, but they are just clouds and they come and go of their own accord. The practitioner is advised to watch them from a distance and allow them to come and go. Then attention is directed to the sky itself, the space within which these clouds move. To finish, attention is directed back to the breathing, to reground the practitioner in the body.

This activity was extended to include another metaphor for thought, that of waves in the ocean. The practitioner begins with the ocean and then focuses on the waves, in whatever form they occur, and then returns awareness to the ocean, having noticed that once a wave disappears, it leaves nothing behind.

A final activity focused on the feeling tone of thoughts. The central question here is, “What do thoughts feel like?” Does the practitioner enjoy them or want them to go away? The practitioner is asked to notice the feeling associated with the thought and to name it. Finally, the practitioner is asked if she can notice the space between thoughts, and whether it is still and peaceful there.

Family Loving-Kindness Exercise This is a family practice that extends mindfulness from a solitary to a social activity, and is designed to bring the whole family together. Members sit together and speak according to the following rules. A stick or similar object is passed around, and whoever holds the stick can speak without interruption from anyone else. Everyone else just listens, nodding their heads to indicate that they really are listening. Each person speaks of a time when they felt hurt by others; and then a time when they hurt others, and how they feel about that. When everyone is finished, each participant makes a drawing illustrating their own hurt and that of others, and places the drawings into a bowl at the centre of the circle. The drawings are taken and thrown away, thus throwing away our own hurts and those of others.

Meditation on Anger/Worry This is a guided meditation that was developed during the practice period as an extension of mindfulness skills for those children who may find it suitable, based on the assessment of their mother teacher. Like Meditation on the Soles of the Feet (SoF) (Singh, Wahler, Adkins, & Myers, 2003), its purpose is to allow the child practitioner a safe environment within which he can practise mindfulness of disturbing emotion, so that when such an emotion arises in life he will be prepared to use it as an object of mindfulness. The practitioner relaxes in a sitting or supine posture, then places his hands on his stomach to feel the movements associated with breathing. She then remembers a situation in which she was angry or worried, and allows herself to feel the emotion evoked. Then, she lets go of the memory and returns to the simple presence of the movements in the stomach associated with breathing.

Mindfulness Meditation Itself The oldest child participant, David, was 15, and after an initial session in which he was introduced to the five basic activities he was asked if he would like to bypass these exercises and simply be taught the meditation practice in the same way as his mother. He agreed to this, and the training unfolded with particular attention to working with the physical challenge of simply sitting still, which was very difficult for him, combined with the mental challenge of remaining present to whatever was arising for him.

5.3 Delivery of IM Programme

5.3.1 Intervention Methods

To meet the wide range of the children’s learning readiness and requirements, the intervention used the principles of UDL and differentiation. Differentiation of learning content began with individual interviews prior to the parent-implemented child mindfulness training. The interviews built an understanding of each individual child participant that assisted design of the initial mindfulness activities. Differentiation continued with the conduct of weekly home visits and online sessions during the training period, and with modifications of mindfulness exercises or creation of new ones wherever individual circumstances suggested this would be useful.

The principles of self-determination and the pedagogical practice of visual modelling guided differentiation of the learning process. The five basic activities (Appendix 1) were video-recorded and inserted into an iPad app that allowed children to name the mindfulness programme according to their preferences. Parents and children were encouraged to practise together as frequently as possible so as to make mindfulness exercises a part of their family life. They also had the option of deciding both the type of mindfulness activity they wanted to practise, and the time during which they practised it.

5.3.2 *Intervention Procedure*

The parent-implemented home-based child mindfulness intervention consisted of a 3-week training period and a one-year practice period. The intervention began in February 2013, with three weekly home visits to support the six mother teachers deliver the mindfulness intervention to their child. After each home visit, mothers were invited to participate in an online session to discuss any adjustments to the training content and methods. Mothers and children were encouraged to continue with regular practice until February 2014. During this 12-month practice period, online group meetings, face-to-face group meetings and social media supported the practice of mothers and children.

5.3.2.1 Intervention Period

The intervention plan was developed prior to the three weekly individual home visits. The aims of the first home visit and online meeting were to introduce the five mindfulness activities and to set homework, so mother teachers and their children could practise the activities as part of their daily routine. An early instance of feedback was the unexpected result that all child learners experienced physical tiredness after practising the mindfulness activities that involved moving their arm (i.e. Fig. 8 and Waving), because of tightness and weakness in their shoulder area. The second and third visits, along with follow-up online meetings with mother teachers, allowed the process of identifying any necessary adjustments of the intervention content and methods to continue.

Vicky requested new activities that could address Sam's tendency to be entangled with negative thoughts and worry, along with an activity that could be used for the whole family. This led to the development of the mindfulness of mind and family loving-kindness exercises (Appendix 2). As we have seen, David, the oldest child participant, chose to bypass the initial mindfulness exercises once he had been introduced to them, and to simply learn mindfulness meditation in the same way as his mother. In contrast John, the youngest participant, quickly mastered these five basic activities and from the second session began to practise them independently at school to calm down his agitation.

5.3.2.2 Practice Period

During the practice period, mother teachers and their child practitioners were supported by a variety of social media (Facebook, Skype and Google Hangouts) and face-to-face meetings. Facebook was employed to create a sense of social cohesion among the mothers, providing a place where they could share their trials and triumphs in their mindfulness teaching and practice, as well as their everyday social events. Online meetings allowed mothers the satisfaction of visual real-time contact. At first Skype was used, then Google Hangouts. These meetings further strengthened the social bonds between mothers and the authors and served as virtual mindfulness meditation meetings, where all participants could meditate silently together. These ongoing group conversations highlighted the need for a new mindfulness activity to address children's anger and worry. The guided meditation on anger/worry was developed as a response.

An additional benefit of these meetings emerged when children would occasionally join their mothers. Seeing other children practising meditation stimulated their interest and helped to normalise their own practice. The virtual meetings inspired the mothers to join together with their children in face-to-face meetings with the authors and each other during school holidays. These were family outings that included a range of social contacts as well as a group meditation session. Participation in online and face-to-face meetings was voluntary. Of the six families, three participated regularly.

5.3.3 Engagement in Mindfulness Practice

The results of the systematic review of mindfulness interventions highlighted the importance of long-term practice to generate long-lasting effects, such as behavioural and psychological wellbeing, for individuals with developmental disabilities (Hwang & Kearney, 2013). Long-term practice presupposes a firm willingness to engage with mindfulness training, something not readily expected from children with ASD since they typically present with low levels of engagement in learning (Keen, 2010). The following sections focus on the nature of the engagement demonstrated by the six mother–child dyads. We review qualitative data drawn from online group conversations through Facebook and in face-to-face meetings that indicate the level and characteristics of engagement in mindfulness practice.

5.3.3.1 Mother and Child Both Engaged: Vicky–Sam

Vicky and Sam demonstrated an active and ongoing engagement in mindfulness practice. They both recognised the occasions they needed it. On 6 March 2013, Sam told his mother, "I need to calm my head", and practised two mindfulness activities. Vicky was taken by surprise by Sam's capacity to recognise his buzzing thoughts and meditated together with him to help him release them. Vicky sometimes expressed the need for regularity in their mindfulness practice. She wrote on 2 April 2013, "the wheels have fallen off the mindfulness wagon this past week. Tonight Sam was going through a rough moment being stuck in his own negative thought pattern. We sat and spoke about what he was thinking and how it made him feel. We then did three different mind gym exercises and he was so much more relaxed. Now to put the wheels back on my wagon also".

Vicky and Sam did not participate in online and face-to-face meetings during the practice period. Although Vicky tried to persuade him to join in, Sam found it "too weird". They continued with home practice instead, working on the family loving-kindness exercise and meditation on anger/worry. When the project was formally completed in February 2014, Vicky wrote that teaching her son mindfulness "has been difficult and rewarding. Sam has been reluctant to learn and practise mindfulness from the start. During the project he surprised me by taking part as it became a ritual for him. We had some breakthroughs".

5.3.3.2 Mother and Child Both Engaged: Diana–John

John mastered all five mindfulness activities at the first session and kept in practice by instructing his family in them. Diana wrote on 10 February 2013, "John is embracing the calm and instilling it in those around him this weekend". He proclaimed, "Stay calm mum, take a deep breath and breath out the anger. Now tell me how do you feel!" On 12 March 2013, she wrote that John continued to enjoy "spontaneous mind gym and instructing the family", and his other siblings began to instruct their parents to be mindful. Diana and her children, including John, participated in a majority of the online meetings and in all face-to-face meetings. When the intervention was formally closed in February 2014, Diana noted that John's aggressive behaviour had become "significantly reduced" during the intervention period, although she felt that other factors, such as his developing maturity, may have played a role. She also noticed that when he got upset, he could self-manage the situation more readily.

5.3.3.3 Mother and Child Both Engaged: Mariam–Peter

Mariam and Peter also regularly participated in online and face-to-face meetings during the practice period. From the beginning, Mariam found it difficult to engage Peter in regular practice of mindfulness activities. Mariam and the authors tried to make his practice commitment more visible and concrete by encouraging him to place a pebble into a jar each time he practised a mindfulness activity, with the promise that he would get a reward when the jar was filled up. On 7 March 2013 she wrote, "I feel like I have been constantly putting out Peter's firebomb anxiety attacks recently. Engaging Peter in meditation has also been a challenge. He does, however, enjoy a Lying Lion in bed at night with us squashed in the bed together. He can recite the dialogue and especially likes the 'Smile and thank yourself' at the end".

In another note, made on 23 July 2013, Mariam illustrated the calming effect that online group meditation had on Peter's anxiety. That day Peter experienced a series of frustrations when the home computer, his laptop and his iPad all malfunctioned. Mariam and her partner anticipated "a long night of angst of being repeatedly let down". To their surprise, Peter voluntarily joined in the online meeting and then quietly went to sleep. In February 2014 Mariam described how they have practised mindfulness together. "I try to incorporate breathing meditation as we drive to school each day. We spend time listening to music together as a way of freeing Peter's mind of worrying thoughts on a daily basis".

5.3.3.4 Mother Engaged, Child Disengaged: Molly–Casey

Molly saw the benefits of practising mindfulness for herself and this made her highly motivated to continue with her own practice and teach it to her son, Casey. "I find the quality of what I do increases dramatically whenever I do it mindfully. I am present to the experience, whatever that experience may be (pleasant or otherwise). When I listen mindfully to someone, I really listen and they can feel it (my kids love it when I do this)". However, she found it challenging to engage Casey in mindfulness activities. Prior to the child mindfulness intervention he was excited about learning mindfulness meditation and even asked his mother to get him a meditation stool. As identified from the individual interviews, Casey was interested in listening to and making sounds. After the first session, Molly and Casey purchased a singing bowl to practise the Meditation on Sound.

His enthusiasm, however, quickly waned. Molly wrote that he became "totally uninterested" (14 February 2013). Molly kept inviting Casey to practise mindfulness together with her, but without forcing him. She practised in front of her three children so Casey could be more exposed to the activities. She found instead that her other two children, who are also on the autism spectrum, joined her, and she saw subsequent improvements in her relationship with them, such as a new physical closeness with her youngest child. At one point Molly wrote of having Casey listen to the guided meditation files to stimulate his interest, because of his interest in sounds (4 March 2013). However, during a subsequent group meeting she reported that this effort failed, although she continued to think that sound would be the gateway into mindfulness for Casey.

Molly did note that Casey was able to articulate his uncontrollable urge to chew things when he felt nervous (22 March 2013). Also, Casey occasionally joined the online meetings, and he attended all the face-to-face meetings along with his mother and siblings. In these meetings he did not, however, fully participate in the group meditation. In February 2014 Molly's conclusion when she looked back to the child mindfulness intervention period was, "It has helped him by helping me be more mindful and giving me more peace".

5.3.3.5 Mother and Child Engaged and Then Disengaged: Shane–David

At the beginning of the parent-implemented child mindfulness intervention, both Shane and David were highly motivated in their mindfulness practice. David chose to bypass the activities designed for children and to learn the same practice that was taught to his mother. They participated in online group meditation meetings until May 2013, when Shane became physically unwell. Although up to then she had been strongly committed to her mindfulness practice, once she fell sick she struggled to maintain her engagement with both her normal duties and her delivery of the parent-implemented mindfulness intervention. David's interest in and commitment to mindfulness meditation subsided along with Shane's.

5.3.3.6 Mother and Child Both Disengaged: Sally–Bindy

Despite her best wishes, during the parent mindfulness training period Sally struggled to find time to engage with the practice, and during the parent-implemented child mindfulness intervention period she continued to find it difficult to make time to teach mindfulness activities to her daughter. Sally and Bindy did not participate in any online or face-to-face meetings, except for the final face-to-face meeting in February 2014, which was held to formally close the project.

During the three home visit sessions Bindy learned the mindfulness activities through verbal instruction combined with visual modelling, despite the limitations in her expressive language. She practised them with beaming smiles. Little opportunity, however, was provided for her to continue with mindfulness activities during the following practice period. Unlike other mother teachers, Sally did not share her teaching experience at the online community space, and at the closing meeting she spoke of her lack of opportunity to practise mindfulness activities with her daughter. Of the six mother–child dyads, Sally–Bindy was the only one that did not complete the parent-implemented child mindfulness intervention.

5.3.3.7 Observations

This review of the patterns of engagement in mindfulness practice of the six mother–child dyads yields the following observations. When mothers were engaged in mindfulness teaching and practice, their children may or may not be engaged in mindfulness practice. When mothers were disengaged from mindfulness teaching and practice, their children were also disengaged from practice. These patterns may reflect the characteristics of people with ASD, who typically display low levels of engagement in learning (Keen, 2010). They may also reflect the design of the parent-implemented intervention. Intervention results rely on parents fulfilling their teaching role, without which it cannot be expected that children will be engaged in learning mindfulness activities.

A key to engagement in mindfulness practice is, as Molly said, seeing the benefits of practising mindfulness for the practitioners themselves. To see the benefits of practising mindfulness, however, a sustained engagement is required. As discussed in Chap. 3, this situation demonstrates the role of effort in the practice of mindfulness. People will not make an effort to practise mindfulness unless they think it is worthwhile, but cannot know it is worthwhile until they make the effort to practise it.

5.3.4 Teacher Quality and Intervention Fidelity

Teacher quality is a major element in determining the level of engagement in mindfulness practice for children with ASD, and can help determine the success or otherwise of a mindfulness intervention. Mindfulness teachers of individuals with DD need an understanding of disability as well as intellectual and experiential knowledge of mindfulness (Hwang & Kearney, 2013). The engagement patterns that emerged from the review of the six mother–child dyads, for example, indicated that teachers must embody mindfulness practice if they are to enhance the level of engagement in teaching and learning mindfulness (Grossman, 2010).

To ensure intervention fidelity of the parent-implemented child mindfulness training, we followed the same steps that were conducted to establish fidelity of the parent mindfulness training (see *4.3.4 Teacher Quality and Intervention Fidelity*) along with an additional intervention focus, that of supporting mother teachers to increase their independence in their teaching role. In the beginning of the intervention period, mother teachers played the role of co-teacher along with the authors. As the intervention progressed, mother teachers gradually became the primary teacher.

To ensure intervention fidelity we, the developers of the mindfulness activities, supported mothers in delivering the training to their children. Prior to each weekly home visit, learning plans were developed with learning objectives, activities and pedagogy. The majority of home-based training sessions were videoed, except in the case of one child who did not want to be recorded. A researcher in psychology, who is independent of this study and familiar with mindfulness practice, examined video footage of three randomly selected child mindfulness-training sessions using the intervention fidelity checklist we developed following Smith, Daunic and Taylor (2007). Fidelity measured against the checklist demonstrated 100 % fidelity.

5.3.5 *Data Collection and Analysis*

The same measures that were used to examine the effects of the parent mindfulness training were adopted to investigate the effects of the parent-implemented child mindfulness training. The effects of the child mindfulness training were explored first for the children who underwent the training and then for the mothers who delivered it. We conducted a paired-sample Wilcoxon signed rank test to identify the training effects at a group level. For the training effects of children, we examined changes detected in children's problem behaviour, using the CBCL scale rated by their mothers. For the mothers, we examined changes in their levels of mindfulness, family quality of life and parenting stress, as indicated on the associated scales. To develop a broad picture of the mindfulness intervention effects, we also looked at the differences before and after parental training, and after child training. We then studied any changes reported for individual mother–child dyads at the conclusion of the parent-implemented mindfulness training.

5.4 Effects of IM Programme

5.4.1 *Intervention Effects for Children*

Figure 5.1 presents the Total Problems scores of the CBCL scales that the six mothers rated as global indices of their children's problems for the three stages before the parent mindfulness training (P1), after the parent mindfulness training (P2), and after the parent-implemented child mindfulness training (P3). The comparisons between the Total Problems scores between P2 and P3 suggest possible effects of the parent-implemented child mindfulness training. Of the five mothers who delivered the mindfulness intervention to their children, four reported reductions in the scores. Sam demonstrated reductions in the Total Problems scores from 54 at P2 to 29 at P3. John's scores were reduced from 77 at P2 to 52 at P3. Although reductions reported for Peter and Casey were smaller than those for Sam and John, Peter and Casey also showed reductions in their Total Problems scores from 78 to 75 and 85 to 76, respectively. For David, however, there was an increase in Total Problems scores, from 77 at P2 to 86 at P3.

Chapter 4 examined changes in the children's problem behaviours from P1 to P2, and in this section we will re-examine these results along with changes from P2 to P3, to give a broader picture of the results of the mindfulness intervention for both parents and children. Reductions in the Total Problems scores between P1 and P2 were reported for all children with the exception of Casey. This illustrates that the children may have benefited from the parent mindfulness intervention even though it did not involve training them in mindfulness. Following these reductions, further reductions from P2 to P3 were reported for Sam, John and Peter. No child

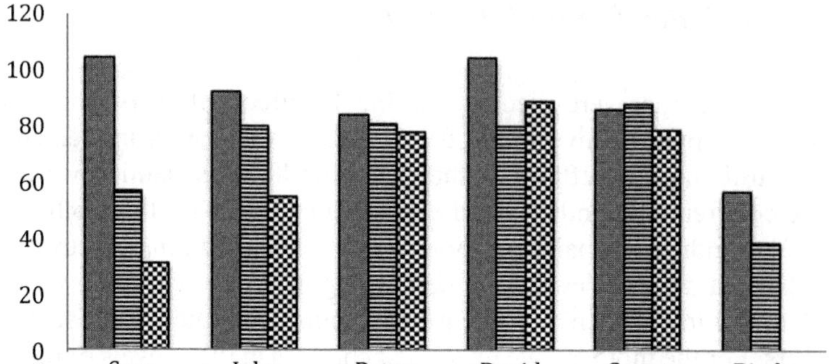

	Sam	John	Peter	David	Casey	Bindy
P1	101	89	81	101	83	54
P2	54	77	78	77	85	36
P3	29	52	75	86	76	

Fig. 5.1 CBCL total problems scores reported for children at P1, P2 and P3

demonstrated increased problem behaviour at the conclusion of the parent-implemented child mindfulness training in comparison with P1. However, fluctuations in the Total Problems scores from P1 to P3 were noticed for David and Casey. In addition, the Total Problems scores for Bindy at P3 are unknown. These results, along with an increase reported for David between P2 and P3, warrant discussion in relation to the issue of engagement with mindfulness practice.

There are nine areas in the CBCL scales that describe different aspects of challenging behavioural issues. Comparing before (P2) and after (P3) the parent-implemented child mindfulness training, at P3, mothers noticed reductions in their child's problem behaviours in relation to thought problems, anxious/depressed, aggressive behaviour and attention problems (Fig. 5.2). Mothers most frequently noted reductions in the areas of thought problems and anxious/depressed. For example, reductions in thought problems were observed for Sam, John, Peter and David, and reductions in anxious/depressed for Sam, John, Peter and Casey. Following the parent-implemented child mindfulness training, the mothers of Sam, John and Peter reported decreases in externalising problems (i.e. rule-breaking and aggressive behaviour) for their children.

The comparisons of children's problem behaviour from P1 to P2, as explored in Chap. 3, illustrated areas (i.e. anxious/depressed, aggressive behaviour, attention problems and thought problems) in which children with ASD may have benefitted from parent mindfulness training without themselves undergoing the training. The comparisons of children's problem behaviour across P1, P2 and P3 demonstrate incremental reductions in children's problem behaviour. The reductions in problem behaviour (e.g. thought problems and anxious/depressed) from P1 to P2, and further reductions from P2 to P3, together suggest the importance of training both children themselves and their parents in mindfulness.

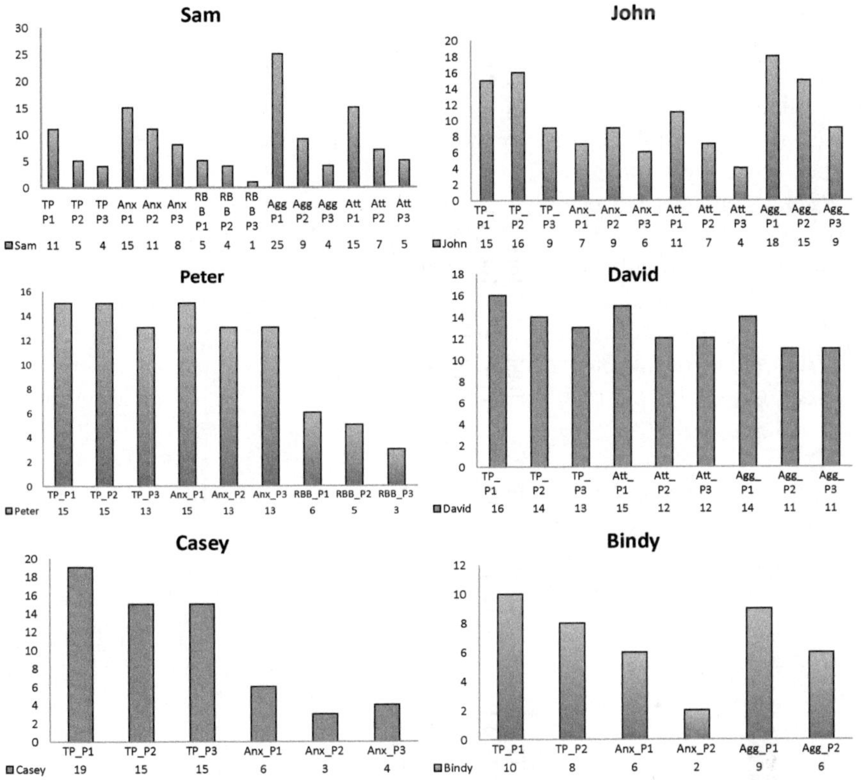

Fig. 5.2 Effects of Mindfulness interventions for children at P1, P2 and P3 in the areas of thought problems (*TP*), anxious/depressed (*Anx*), attention problems (*Att*), aggressive behaviour (*Agg*), and rule-breaking behaviour (*RBB*)

We conducted a paired-sample Wilcoxon signed rank test to explore the effects of mindfulness training for the children at a group level. As presented in Table 5.3, a consistent pattern was noticed in children's problem behaviour. At the conclusion of parent mindfulness training (P2), some noticeable reductions were found in children's anxious/depressed ($z=1.897$, $n=6$, $p=0.058$) and thought problems ($z=1.761$, $n=6$, $p=0.078$). Although further reductions were noted between P2 and P3, no statistical significance was found. The only comparisons with statistical significance between P1 and P3 were reductions in children's anxious/depressed ($z=2.060$, $n=5$, $p=0.039$) and thought problems ($z=2.023$, $n=5$, $p=0.043$). Although not identical, a similar pattern was reported for children's total problems scores, with reductions reported at the conclusion of parent mindfulness training (P2) ($z=1.992$, $n=6$, $p=0.046$) and at the conclusion of parent-implemented child mindfulness training (P3) ($z=2.023$, $n=5$, $p=0.043$). This suggests the potentiality of mindfulness interventions as a way of supporting families living with ASD and challenging behaviour as a unit.

Table 5.3 Effects of Mindfulness interventions for children

	Anx_P2—Anx_P1	Anx_P3-Anx_P1	Anx_P3-Axn_P2	TP_P2—TP_P1	TP_P3—TP_P1	TP_P3—TP_P2	Total_P2—Total_P1	Total_P3—Total_P1	Total_P3—Total_P2
Z	−1.897[a]	−2.060[a]	−0.378[a]	−1.761[a]	−2.023[a]	−1.841[a]	−1.992[a]	−2.023[a]	−1.361[a]
Asymp. Sig. (2-tailed)	0.058	0.039	0.705	0.078	0.043	0.066	0.046	0.043	0.174

[a] Based on positive ranks

5.4.2 Intervention Effects for Mothers

Figure 5.3 presents the levels of mindfulness, parenting stress and family quality of life that mothers rated on the associated scales for the three stages of before the parent mindfulness intervention (P1), after the parent mindfulness intervention (P2), and after the parent-implemented child mindfulness intervention (P3). The comparisons between P1 and P2 indicate the direct effects of the parent mindfulness training for mothers, while those between P2 and P3 indicate the indirect effects for mothers of the child mindfulness training. The comparisons between P1 and P3 represent the overall effects of training the family unit in mindfulness.

The comparisons between P1 and P2, as explored in Chap. 4, indicated overall improvements in the psychological wellbeing of the mothers, as the majority reported increases in mindfulness and decreases in parenting stress. The comparisons between P2 and P3 indicate the possibility of supporting mothers by training their

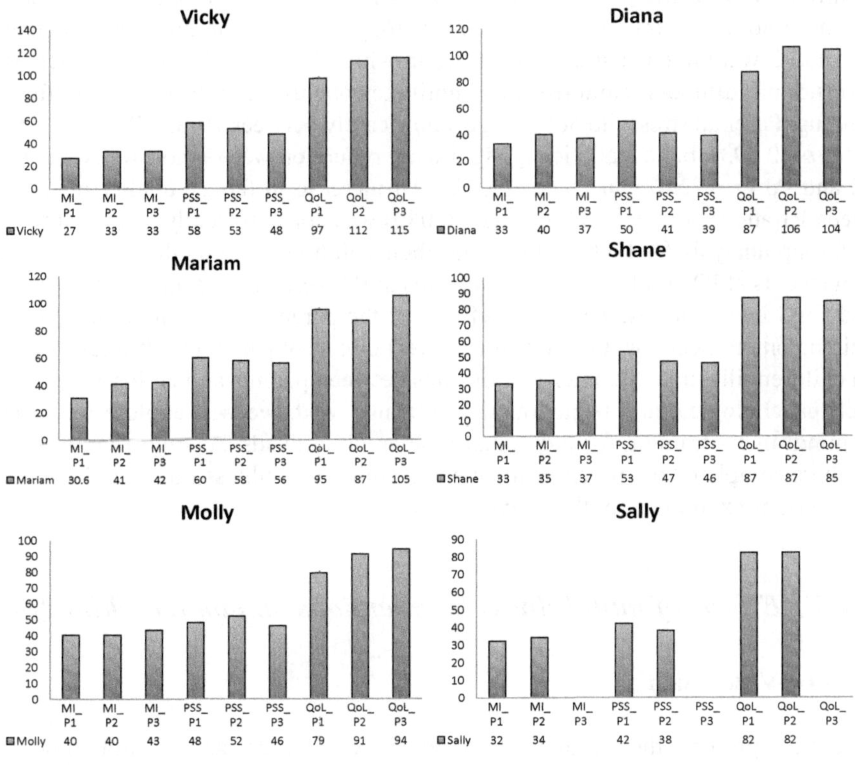

Fig. 5.3 Effects of Mindfulness interventions for mothers at P1, P2 and P3 measured using Mindfulness Inventory (*MI*), Parenting Stress Scale (*PSS*) and Family Quality of Life (QoL)

children in mindfulness, as reductions in parenting stress were found for all five mothers who attempted to deliver mindfulness training to their children. Mariam reported an increase in family quality of life by 18, while Molly and Vicky reported an increase by three. In addition, increases in mindfulness for the period from P2 to P3 were reported for Molly (from 40 to 43), Mariam (from 41 to 42) and Shane (from 35 to 37).

As the parent-implemented child mindfulness training did not include mindfulness training for mothers as such, these changes noted for mothers can be seen in relation to the effects of training others in mindfulness. Alternatively, it could also be understood as the further accumulation of the effects of the initial parent training. In any event, comparisons across P1, P2 and P3 suggest overall incremental improvements, with some fluctuations, in the perceived levels of mindfulness, parenting stress and family quality of life for all mothers.

We also conducted a paired-sample Wilcoxon signed rank test to examine whether or not the differences at the conclusion of parent mindfulness intervention (P2) and parent-implemented child mindfulness intervention (P3) showed any statistical significance at a group level (Table 5.4). Mindfulness levels increased after the parent mindfulness training ($z = -2.032$, $n = 6$, $p = 0.042$). The differences between P2 and P3 were not statistically significant, which indicates these newly increased levels of mindfulness remained stable until the conclusion of the child mindfulness training. Parental stress did not change significantly between P1 and P2 ($z = -1.682$, $n = 6$, $p = 0.093$), but a statistically significant reduction was demonstrated between P2 and P3 ($z = -2.023$, $n = 5$, $p = 0.042$). An increase in family quality of life between P1 and P3 ($z = -1.753$, $n = 5$, $p = 0.080$) was not statistically significant.

Group analysis for both mothers and their children suggests that the initial improvements at P2 and further improvements at P3 were the overall effects of parent and child interventions. The direct effects of the parent-implemented mindfulness training on mothers, together with the indirect effects of parent mindfulness training on children, illustrate the interrelationships between parents and children regarding their psychological and behavioural wellbeing. Next, we will explore the effects of mindfulness training for individual mother–child dyads. As only five of the six mothers completed the parent-implemented child mindfulness training, the following sections examine only these five dyads.

5.4.3 *Effects of mindfulness interventions on mother–child dyads*

5.4.3.1 Vicky–Sam

Figure 5.4 presents the training effects on Vicky, using bar graphs, and on her son Sam, using line graphs, at P1, P2 and P3. Of the three marks on Sam's line graph, the first indicates a score of a corresponding CBCL subscale at P1, the second at P2 and the third at P3. The comparisons between P2 and P3 illustrate the effects of

Table 5.4 Effects of mindfulness interventions for mothers

	P2_MI—P1_MI	P3_MI—P1_MI	P3_MI—P2_MI	P2_PSS—P1_PSS	P3_PSS—P1_PSS	P3_PSS—P2_PSS	P2_QoL—P1_QoL	P3_QoL—P1_QoL	P3_QoL—P2_QoL
Z	−2.032[a]	−2.032[a]	−0.552[a]	−1.682[b]	−2.023[b]	−2.032[b]	−1.461[a]	−1.753[a]	−1.225[a]
Asymp. Sig. (2-tailed)	0.042	0.042	0.581	0.093	0.043	0.042	0.144	0.080	0.221

[a] Based on negative ranks
[b] Based on positive ranks

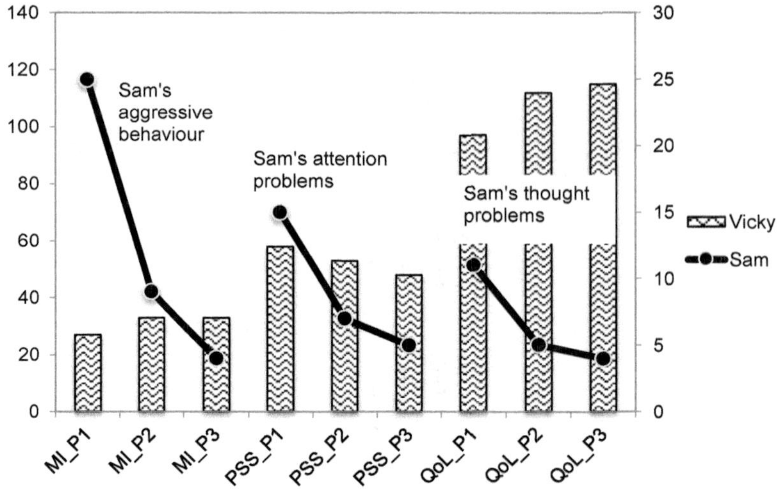

Fig. 5.4 Effects of Mindfulness interventions for Vicky and Sam at P1, P2 and P3

parent-implemented mindfulness training for Sam as reported by Vicky. They include reductions in his aggressive behaviour, attention problems and thought problems. During this period, she also noticed reductions in her parenting stress and increases in her family quality of life. These results suggest that Sam's mindfulness training may have influenced Vicky's psychological wellbeing. Alternatively, they may reflect the continued effects of Vicky's practice from the parent mindfulness intervention.

A mutual influence between Vicky's psychological wellbeing and Sam's behavioural wellbeing was indicated across P1, P2 and P3. At the conclusion of the parent mindfulness intervention (P2), she reported increases in her mindfulness from 27 at P1 to 33, and family quality of life from 97 at P1 to 112. These were accompanied by substantial reductions in Sam's problem behaviour. For example, she reported reductions for Sam in aggressive behaviour from 25 (clinical range) at P1 to 10 (normal range) at P2, and attention problems from 15 (clinical range) at P1 to seven (normal range) at P2. The indirect effects of parent mindfulness training on Sam at P2 and those of parent-implemented child mindfulness training on Vicky at P3 suggest the mutual benefits a mother and her child may receive from working together on a joint mindfulness project. Once more, however, the cumulative linear effects of Vicky's mindfulness training could also be a factor.

5.4.3.2 Diana–John

The second dyad, Diana and John, also demonstrated mutuality in the benefits they gained from mindfulness practice. At P3, Diana reported reductions for John in aggressive behaviour, attention problems and thought problems (Fig. 5.5). For ex-

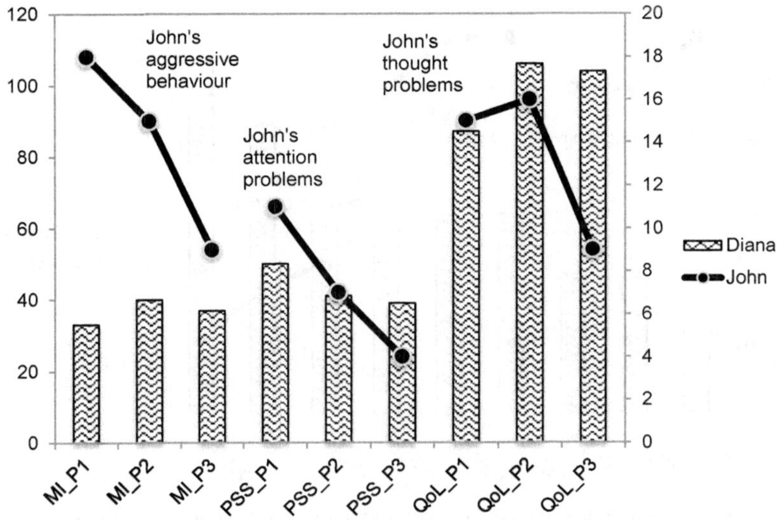

Fig. 5.5 Effects of mindfulness interventions for Diana and John at P1, P2 and P3

ample, his aggressive behaviour was reduced from 15 (borderline clinical range) at P2 to nine (normal range) at P3, and his thought problems from 16 (clinical range) at P2 to nine (clinical range) at P3. For herself, at P3 Diana reported slight decreases in mindfulness and family quality of life, but also in her level of parenting stress, while at P2 she reported improvements in her levels of mindfulness, parenting stress and family quality of life, along with reductions in aggressive behaviour and attention problems for John.

5.4.3.3 Mariam–Peter

The results of the third dyad, Mariam and her son Peter, are again suggestive of mutual influences between parent and child throughout the mindfulness intervention. At P3 Mariam reported reductions in Peter's thought problems and rule-breaking behaviour, accompanied by an increase in family quality of life and reduction in parenting stress for her (Fig. 5.6). At P2 she reported an increase in mindfulness, although not in parenting stress and family quality of life, for herself. At the same time she noticed slight reductions in her son's rule-breaking and aggressive behaviour.

5.4.3.4 Molly–Casey

The fourth dyad, made up of Molly and Casey, also lends support for the mutuality of the relationships between parent and child at P2, when Molly reported improvements in her levels of parenting stress and family quality of life, along with reduc-

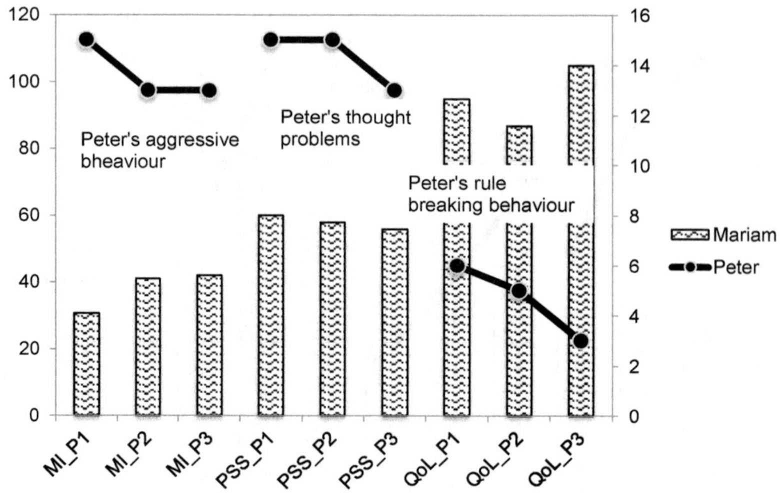

Fig. 5.6 Effects of mindfulness interventions for Mariam and Peter at P1, P2 and P3

tions in thought problems and anxiety problems for Casey (Fig. 5.7). Unlike the previous three dyads, however, at P3 Molly did not find any positive differences in Casey's problem behaviour. While it remained less at P3 compared with P1, his anxiety slightly increased between P2 and P3, from 3 to 4. Molly reported improvements in her psychological wellbeing at P3, as demonstrated by slight increases in her levels of mindfulness and family quality of life, and a decrease in parenting stress.

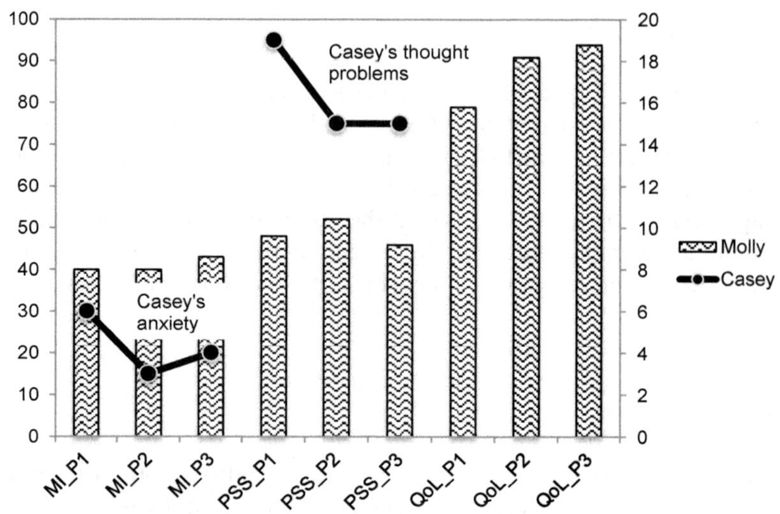

Fig. 5.7 Effects of mindfulness interventions for Molly and Casey at P1, P2 and P3

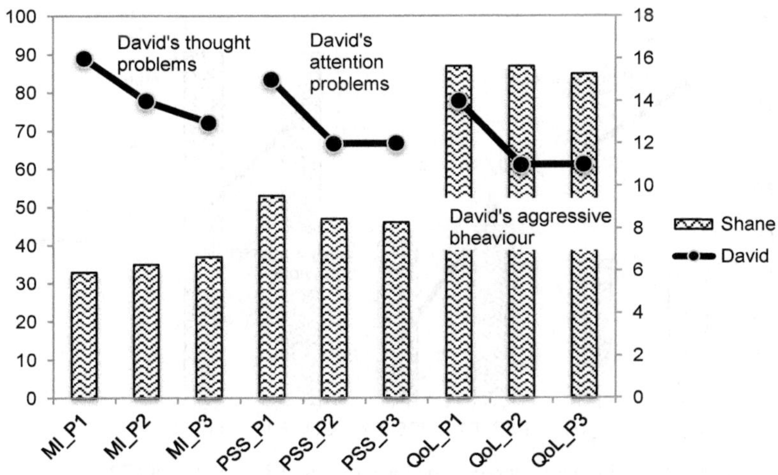

Fig. 5.8 Effects of mindfulness interventions for Shane and David at P1, P2 and P3

5.4.3.5 Shane–David

The Shane–David dyad demonstrated a similar pattern to that of Molly–Casey, with a clearer mutual influence between mother and child at P2 than at P3. Overall, Shane and David demonstrated improvements in their psychological and behavioural wellbeing at P3 compared with those at P1 (Fig. 5.8). At P3, however, Shane did not find noticeable differences in David's problem behaviour from P2 except for his thought problems, while she reported a slight increase in her level of mindfulness and slight decreases in her levels of parenting stress and family quality of life. At P2 Shane had demonstrated improvements in her levels of mindfulness, parenting stress and family quality of life, along with reductions in thought problems, attention problems and aggressive behaviour for David.

5.4.3.6 Sally–Bindy

As indicated earlier, Sally did not complete the parent-implemented child mindfulness intervention. Figure 5.9 therefore indicates a mutual influence between mother and child at P2, when an improvement in psychological wellbeing was reported for Sally at the conclusion of parent mindfulness training, along with an improvement in behavioural wellbeing for Bindy.

5.4.4 Conclusion

In this chapter we presented stage 2 of the mindfulness intervention, that of parent-implemented mindfulness training for the six children with ASD and challenging

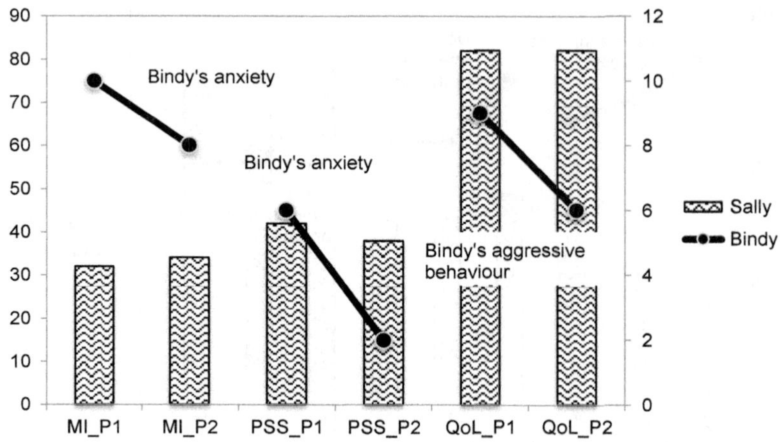

Fig. 5.9 Effects of mindfulness interventions for Sally and Bindy at P1 and P2

behaviours. This stage began with a process of getting to know the individual characters of the children through individual interviews, on the basis of which we developed four basic mindfulness activities that focused on the movements of the body and one activity that focused on listening to sounds. The exercises were provisional only and subject to amendment or extension by mother teachers. Three more exercises were developed during the training in response to feedback from mother teachers, and these extended the scope the mindfulness practice to the mind and emotions.

The children's training began with three weekly home visits by the researchers assisted by the mothers, after which the mothers took over as the primary teachers. Online and face-to-face meetings were held to support mothers and children during their training. We found that the children depended on the engagement of their mothers to stimulate their own commitment, although this was not necessarily enough to keep them engaged.

Overall, the results showed gradual improvements in the psychological wellbeing of the mothers and the behavioural wellbeing of the children, from P1 at the beginning of the intervention to P3 at its conclusion. They also indicated the complex connections between mothers and children that emerged in the patterns of direct and indirect results.

For example, at P2, the end of the mother's mindfulness training, mothers overall reported increased mindfulness with statistical significance and decreased stress but without statistical significance. Their children, meanwhile, demonstrated statistically significant reductions in their Total Problems scores. However, these effects on the children were indirect, possibly the result of changes undergone by their mothers as they practised mindfulness. At P3, the conclusion of the children's training, they continued to progress with their Total Problems scores, apparently as the direct result of their mindfulness training. Specifically, they demonstrated statistically significant reductions in anxiety and thought problems, which had been reduced at P2 but without statistical significance. Their mothers also continued to progress, in terms of statistically significant reductions in parenting stress. At the end of the training, mother and child demonstrated the full effects of the mindfulness intervention together, as a single unit. Overall, we can say that the benefits of mindfulness practice accrued to the mother–child dyad, rather than the individual mother or child.

Was the progress that was presented by the mothers during their child's training the direct result of their continued mindfulness practice? Or was it at least partly the indirect effects of their child's practice? Whatever the answer to this question, these patterns outlined above demonstrate the web of interdependency that binds mother and child, and this in turn indicates the potentiality of applying mindfulness training to family or school settings where the bonds of community may strengthen the effects of individual mindfulness practice.

References

American Psychiatric Association. (2013). *Diagnostic and statistical manual of mental disorders* (5th ed.). Arlington: American Psychiatric Publishing.

Bellini, S., & Akullian, J. (2007). A meta-analysis of video modeling and video self-modeling interventions for children and adolescents with autism spectrum disorders. *Exceptional Children, 73,* 264–287.

Bodhi, B. (Ed.). (2000). *Abhidhammattha Sangaha. A comprehensive manual of abhidhamma.* Seattle: BPS Pariyatti.

Brantlinger, E., Jimenez, R., Klingner, J., Pugach, M., & Richardson, V. (2005). Qualitative studies in special education. *Exceptional Children, 71,* 195–207.

Braun, V., & Clarke, V. (2006). Using thematic analysis in psychology. *Qualitative Research in Psychology, 3,* 77–101.

CAST. (2013). Transforming education through universal design for learning. http://www.cast.org/. Accessed 20 Nov 2014.

Charlop-Christy, M. H., Le, L., & Freeman, K. A. (2000). A comparison of video modeling with in vivo modeling for teaching children with autism. *Journal of Autism and Developmental Disorders, 30,* 537–552.

Coyne, P., Pisha, B., Dalton, B., Zeph, L. A., & Smith, N. C. (2010). Literacy by design: A universal design for learning approach for students with significant intellectual disabilities. *Remedial and Special Education*. doi:10.1177/0741932510381651.

Delano, M. E. (2007). Video modeling interventions for individuals with autism. *Remedial and Special Education, 28,* 33–42.

Eisenhower, A. S., Baker, B. L., & Blacher, J. (2005). Preschool children with intellectual disability: Syndrome specificity, behavior problems, and maternal well-being. *Journal of Intellectual Disability Research, 49,* 657–671.

Grossman, P. (2010). Mindfulness for psychologists: Paying kind attention to the perceptible. *Mindfulness, 1,* 87–97.

Happé, F., Ronald, A., & Plomin, R. (2006). Time to give up on a single explanation for autism. *Nature Neuroscience, 9*(10), 1218–1220.

Harper, A., Dyches, T. T., Harper, J., Roper, S. O., & South, M. (2013). Respite care, marital quality, and stress in parents of children with autism spectrum disorders. *Journal of Autism and Developmental Disorders*. doi:10.1007/s10803-013-1812-0.

Howlin, P., Baron-Cohen, S., & Hadwin, J. (1999). *Teaching children with autism to mind-read: A practical guide for teachers and parents*. London: Wiley.

Hwang, Y.-S. (2014). Miss Mum: Mind and affective experience of Korean learners identified with autism spectrum and cognitive difficulties. *Disability & Society*. doi:10.1080/09687599.2014.958434.

Hwang, Y. S., & Kearney, P. (2013). A systematic review of mindfulness intervention for individuals with developmental disabilities: Long-term practice and long lasting effects. *Research in Developmental Disabilities, 34,* 314–326.

Hwang, Y.-S., Klieve, H., Kearney, P., & Saggers, B. (2013). Experience, recursive awareness and understanding in autism spectrum disorders: Insights of parents and teachers in Singapore. *Asia Pacific Journal of Education*. doi:10.1080/02188791.2013.860013.

Kaiser, A. P., & Hancock, T. B. (2003). Teaching parents new skills to support their young children's development. *Infants & Young Children, 16,* 9–21.

Keen, D. (2010). Engagement of children with autism in learning. *Australasian Journal of Special Education, 33*(2), 130–140.

Keller, D., & Honig, A. S. (2004). Maternal and Paternal Stress in Families With School-Aged Children With Disabilities. *American Journal of Orthopsychiatry, 74*(3), 337–348.

Lee, S. H., Wehmeyer, M. L., Palmer, S. B., Soukup, J. H., & Little, T. D. (2008). Self-determination and access to the general education curriculum. *The Journal of Special Education, 42,* 91–107.

Lewis, S. G., & Batts, K. (2005). How to implement differentiated instruction? *Journal of Staff Development, 26*(4), 26–31.

Mahoney, G., & Wiggers, B. (2007). The Role of parents in early intervention: Implication for social work. *Children and Schools, 29*(1), 7–15.

Matson, M., Mahan, S., & Matson, J. (2009). Parent training: A review of methods for children with autism spectrum disorders. *Research in Autism Spectrum Disorders, 3,* 868–875.

Meo, G. (2008). Curriculum planning for all learners: Applying Universal Design for Learning (UDL) to a high school reading comprehension program. *Preventing School Failure, 52*(2), 21–30.

Nazeer, K. (2006). *Send in the idiots. Stories from the other side of autism*. New York: Bloomsbury.

Nikopoulos, C. K., & Keenan, M. (2007). Using Video Modeling to Teach Complex Social Sequences to Children with Autism. *Journal of Autism and Developmental Disorders, 37,* 678–693.

Oono, I. P., Honey, E. J., & McConachie, H. (2013). Parent-implemented early intervention for young children with autism spectrum disorders (ASD). *Evidence-Based Child Health, 8*(6), 2380–2479.

Rose, D., & Meyer, A. (2002). *Teaching every student in the digital age: Universal design for learning*. Alexandria: ASCD.

Mahasi, S. (1971). *Practical insight meditation. Basic and progressive stages*. Kandy: Buddhist Publication Society.

Schreibman, L., & Ingersoll, B. (2005). Behavioral interventions to promote learning in individuals with autism. In F. Volkmar, R. Paul, R. A. Klin & D. Cohen (Eds.), *Handbook of autism and pervasive developmental disorders* (3rd ed., pp. 882–896). Hoboken: Wiley.

Shogren, K. A., Lopez, S. J., Wehmeyer, M. L., Little, T. D., & Pressgrove, C. L. (2006). The role of positive psychology constructs in predicting life satisfaction in adolescents with and without cognitive disabilities: An exploratory study. *The Journal of Positive Psychology in the Schools, 1,* 37–52.

Silva, L., & Schalock, M. (2012). Autism parenting stress index: Initial psychometric evidence. *Journal of Autism and Developmental Disorders, 42,* 566–574.

Singh, N. N., Wahler, R. G., Adkins, A. D., & Myers, R. E. (2003). Soles of the feet: A mindfulness-based self-control intervention for aggression by an individual with mild mental retardation. *Research in Developmental Disabilities, 24,* 158–169.

Smith, S. W., Daunic, A. P., & Taylor, G. G. (2007). Treatment fidelity in applied educational research: Expanding the adoption and application of measures to ensure evidence-based practice. *Education and treatment of children, 30*(4), 121–134.

Spek, A., van Ham, N., & Nyklicek, I. (2013). Mindfulness-based therapy in adults with an autism spectrum disorder: A randomized controlled trial. *Research in Developmental Disabilities, 34*(1), 246–253.

Tomlinson, C., & Imbeau, M. (2010). *Leading and managing a differentiated classroom*. Alexandria: ASCD.

Udvari-Solner, A., Villa, R., & Thousand, J. (2005). Access to the general education curriculum for all: The universal design process. In R. A. Villa & J. S. Thousand (Eds.), *Creating an inclusive school* (pp. 134–155). Alexandria: ASCD.

Wehmeyer, M. L. (2010). Self-determination. In B. McGaw, E. L. Baker, & P. L. Peterson (Eds.), *International encyclopedia of education* (pp. 857–864). Kidlington: Elsevier Science.

Wehmeyer, M. L. (2011). Assessment and Intervention in Self-Determination *Advances in Learning and Behavioral Disabilities, 24,* 213–249.

Wehmeyer, M. L., & Palmer, S. B. (2003). Adult outcomes from students with cognitive disabilities three years after high school: The impact of self-determination. *Education and Training in Developmental Disabilities, 38,* 131–144.

Wehmeyer, M. L., & Schwartz, M. (1997). Self-determination and positive adult outcomes: A follow up study of youth with mental retardation or learning disabilities. *Exceptional Children, 63,* 245–255.

Wehmeyer, M. L., Shogren, K. A., Palmer, S. B., Williams-Diehm, K. L., Little, T. D., & Boulton, A. (2012). The impact of the self-determined learning model of instruction on student self-determination. *Exceptional Children, 78*(2), 135–153.

West, E. Z., McCollow, M., Gumbarger, G., Kidwell, J., & Cote, D. L. (2013). Current status of evidence-based practice for students with intellectual disability and autism spectrum disorders. *Education and Training in Autism and Developmental Disabilities, 48*(4), 443–455.

White, N., & Hastings, R. P. (2004). Social and professional support for parents of adolescents with severe intellectual disabilities. *Journal of Applied Research in Intellectual Disabilities, 17,* 181–190.

Wong, C., Odom, S. L., Hume, K., Cox, A. W., Fettig, A., Kucharczyk, S., … Schultz, T. R. (2013). *Evidence-based practices for children, youth, and young adults with Autism Spectrum Disorder*. Chapel Hill The University of North Carolina, Frank Porter Graham Child Development Institute, Autism Evidence-Based Practice Review Group.

Wormeli, R. (2006). *Fair isn't always equal: Assessing and grading in the differentiated classroom*. Portland: Stenhouse Publishers.

Chapter 6
Discussion and Conclusion

6.1 Introduction

The defining questions of this study are as follows: (1) what happens to individuals with developmental disabilities (DD) when they practise mindfulness? and (2) what happens to individuals with DD when their family or professional care providers practise mindfulness? We began this investigation by returning to the roots of mindfulness, the Buddha's concept of *sati* found in the Nikāyas, or "collections" of early Buddhist teachings and following its transition into modernity, where the *sati* of the Buddha became the mindfulness of contemporary psychology (Chap. 2). We then conducted a systematic literature review of studies that applied the practice of mindfulness to the behavioural or psychological problems of people with DD (Chap. 3). This review showed that more mindfulness interventions for people with DD were concerned with their behavioural problems rather than their psychological problems, and with individuals with intellectual disabilities (ID) rather than those with autism spectrum disorder (ASD). Hence, the least attention has been given to the psychological problems of people with ASD. While the number of studies addressing this area of need has recently grown, the review demonstrates the need to broaden the scope of mindfulness interventions to address it. Further, the review showed that despite the significant role played by transactional effects in these mindfulness intervention studies (e.g. Neece, 2013; Singh, Lancioni, Winton, Fisher, et al., 2006; Singh et al., 2014), these have not yet been fully explored.

Responding to the lacuna demonstrated by the review, we have conducted a two-stage mindfulness intervention in which stage 1 trained six mothers of children with ASD and challenging behaviours in mindfulness, and stage 2 conducted parent-implemented mindfulness training for these children. The first goal of the stage 1 intervention was to train mothers in mindfulness practice to a level of fluency in their everyday lives. The second goal was to train them to become mindfulness meditation teachers for their own children. The central goal of the stage 2 intervention was to train children with ASD in mindfulness to the degree they could use mindfulness meditation to manage their own challenging behaviours. The results of this two-staged intervention study highlighted both direct and indirect, or

Y.-S. Hwang, P. Kearney, *A Mindfulness Intervention for Children with Autism Spectrum Disorder*, Mindfulness in Behavioral Health,
DOI 10.1007/978-3-319-18962-8_6

transactional effects of mindfulness practice, discussed here in relation to those of previous mindfulness intervention studies (6.2).

This chapter also discusses the theoretical, practical and methodological issues that frame this project (6.3). The theoretical issue considered here involves the concept of mindfulness that was drawn upon to guide this study. To ensure both theoretical coherence and flexibility in method, we chose to go back to the Buddha's original concept of *sati*. Another theoretical issue concerns the qualifications, both theoretical and practical, that are appropriate for mindfulness teachers working with families living with DD, and ASD in particular. These qualifications include an understanding of both mindfulness and disability, which suggest the desirability of an interdisciplinary team approach to teaching mindfulness to people with disabilities.

Other issues concern the importance of effective support networks that would help families sustain their mindfulness practice long enough for them to enjoy the benefits that have been shown to come from long-term practice. It is clear that mindfulness practice influences family dynamics and that raises the need to include the family and school environment in the scope of mindfulness interventions. Finally, this chapter addresses the limitations of the current study (6.4) and its implications for future research (6.5).

6.2 Effects of Mindfulness Training

In this section we will address the effects that mindfulness training had on the six mothers of children with ASD and challenging behaviours and the children themselves. First the training of the mothers will be explored, in terms of its direct effects on the mothers themselves and its indirect effects on their children; then the training of the children will be explored, in terms of its direct effects on the children and indirect effects on their mothers.

6.2.1 Parent Mindfulness Training: Direct Effects on Mothers of Children with ASD

The investigation focused on whether training mothers of children with ASD and challenging behaviours in mindfulness improved their levels of mindfulness, parenting stress and quality of family life, and provided mixed results. A major finding was that the level of mindfulness of the mothers increased, and with statistical significance. Here, the concept of mindfulness that guided the training was drawn directly from the origins of the tradition. This finding conformed with those of recent studies that applied mindfulness to family and professional caregivers of individuals with DD. In these studies, the concept of mindfulness that was used had been adapted from the existing MBIs such as mindfulness-based stress reduction (MBSR) (Bazzano et al., 2013; Benn, Akiva, Arel, & Roeser, 2012), mindfulness-based cognitive therapy (MBCT) and dialectical behaviour therapy (DBT) (Ferraioli & Harris, 2013).

In addition, mothers in this study practised mindfulness independently for a month prior to their final training session, to assist them in making a transition to a self-practice period. The increased mindfulness they experienced therefore conforms to the findings of the previous studies that also reported improved use of mindfulness in mothers of children with ASD at the end of a self-practice period (Singh, Lancioni, Winton, Fisher, et al., 2006) and DD (Singh et al., 2007).

Earlier studies also reported reductions in parenting or caring stress in association with mindfulness training for family and professional care providers of individuals with DD (Benn et al., 2012; Blackledge & Hayes, 2006; Bögels, Hellemans, Deursen, Römer, & Meulen, 2013; Ferraioli & Harris, 2013; Neece, 2013; Singh et al., 2014). However, in this study increased mindfulness in mothers was not accompanied by reduced parenting stress. While five of the six mothers in this study did report reductions in parenting stress at the completion of the mindfulness training, this result did not yield statistical significance. Given the small number in the study, it is possible that a slight increase in parenting stress reported by one mother may have contributed to this absence of statistical significance.

Previous studies that reported increased levels of mindfulness also reported increased parenting satisfaction in parents of children with ASD (Singh, Lancioni, Winton, Fisher, et al., 2006) and DD (Singh et al., 2007), increased satisfaction with life in parents of young children with DD (Neece, 2013) and increased levels of satisfaction in professional care providers of individuals with intellectual disability (Singh et al., 2009). However, in this study the improved mindfulness in parents did not translate into improved family quality of life, as of the six mothers only three reported an increased family quality of life after mindfulness training.

The disparity here may be due to the translation from qualitative to quantitative findings and the complexity of the family quality of life scale. While in this study, mothers reported in group discussions and personal reflective diaries overwhelmingly positive experiences regarding family and personal life as they underwent their mindfulness training, these qualitative reports did not translate into quantitative findings. While satisfaction with parenting or with life constitutes one aspect of family quality of life, the family quality of life scale is much more complex, consisting of family interaction, parenting, emotional wellbeing, physical/material wellbeing and disability-related support (Hoffman, Marquis, Poston, Summers, & Turnbull, 2006). It may be that the satisfaction expressed by the mothers was not extensive enough to affect the family quality of life scale, which includes external factors such as material wellbeing and disability-related support.

Another suggestive finding comes from a study that reported the absence of any significant improvement in self-reported quality of life after training children with externalising disorders, including ASD, and their parents in mindfulness (Bögels, Hoogstad, van Dun, de Schutter, & Restifo, 2008). Prior to the training, the children in this study rated their quality of life quite highly, and Bögels and her research team suspected this may have contributed to an absence of an improved rating after their training. In the current study, the mothers also rated their quality of family life highly prior to their mindfulness training, and the absence of a rise in their rating afterwards may indicate the same phenomenon. In any event, the limitations created by the small sample size are also a consideration.

6.2.2 Parent Mindfulness Training: Indirect Effects on Children with ASD

Another major finding of the parent mindfulness training concerned its indirect effects, as shown by reductions in the problem behaviour of their children with ASD before they practised mindfulness for themselves. This raises what the current study sees as a defining question: What happens to individuals with DD when their family or professional care providers practise mindfulness? Although individually there were differences, at a group level mothers reported statistically significant reductions in their child's total problems scores upon the completion of the parent mindfulness training. This result agreed with the previous studies that reported indirect effects on their children of parent mindfulness training. Neece (2013), for example, documented reductions in the attention problems of children with DD after their parents completed the MBSR program. Singh et al. (2014) also observed reductions in challenging behaviours of children with ASD upon the completion of mindfulness-based positive behaviour support provided to their mothers.

Comparable results were also found in mindful parenting interventions, such as reductions in aggressive behaviours of children with ASD (Singh, Lancioni, Winton, Fisher, et al., 2006) and DD (Singh et al., 2007), and reductions in challenging behaviours of children requiring mental health care, including those with ASD (Bögels et al., 2013). In contrast to mindful parenting intervention studies, however, this study did not include any component addressing parenting. Rather, it focused solely on training mothers in mindfulness on the assumption that the best preparation parents can make for benefiting their children through this training is to embody mindfulness through their commitment to their own practice.

Overall, as shown by the systematic review outlined in Chap. 3, there appear to be significant transactional relationships between the behavioural and psychological problems of care recipients on the one hand, and the relationships between them and their care providers on the other. For both parents and professional care providers, the most frequently reported indirect effects of mindfulness training are reductions in the aggressive behaviours of their care recipients, along with increased satisfaction with the quality of the relationships between care providers and care recipients. The key appears to be the quality of interaction between the parties, and this may improve with increased mindfulness in any of them.

Parent training that improves mindfulness also improves parent–child relationships (e.g. Coatsworth, Duncan, Greenberg and Nix, 2010) and child outcomes (e.g. Singh, Lancioni, Winton, Fisher, et al., 2006; Singh et al., 2007). Parents committed to the practice of mindfulness can become more sensitive to their habitual interactions with their children that normally occur with little or no awareness and that often play a critical role in dysfunctional family dynamics (Dumas, 2005). Mindfulness practice also provides parents, who are often depleted from parenting demands made upon them, with an opportunity for self-nourishment which in turn energises their parenting (Bögels et al., 2013; Bögels, Lehtonen, & Restifo, 2010). Mindfulness training may help mothers accept their children unconditionally and interact with them in a manner supported by loving-kindness (Singh et al., 2007) .

6.2.3 Child Mindfulness Training: Direct Effects on Children with ASD

The other defining question of this study is: What happens to individuals with DD when they practise mindfulness? In this study, mother teachers reported, as effects of parent-implemented mindfulness training for children with ASD and challenging behaviours, statistically significant reductions in anxiety and thought problems. This result agrees with earlier studies that applied modified MBIs, such as ACT and MBCT to individuals with DD. They found reductions in anxiety and obsessive thoughts (Brown & Hooper, 2009) and reductions in anxiety (Idusohan-Moizer, Sawicka, Dendle, & Albany, 2013; Spek, van Ham, & Nyklicek, 2013). A similar result was found in the personal experience of a father who taught mindfulness to his twin boys with ASD (Russell, 2011).

Singh, Lancioni, Manikam, et al. (2011) and Singh, Lancioni, Singh, et al. (2011) also adopted a parent-implemented mindfulness training approach and reported substantial reductions in aggression for children with ASD and Asperger's syndrome. Similarly in this study, out of the five mothers who completed delivery of the parent-implemented child mindfulness training, four reported reductions in aggressive behaviour for their child during the period from before the parent mindfulness training to after the child mindfulness training. These effects differed depending on the individual child–parent dyads. This result will be discussed in relation to the issue of mindfulness teacher quality and the level of engagement in mindfulness practice (6.3.2) .

6.2.4 Child Mindfulness Training: Indirect Effects on Mothers of Children with ASD

At the completion of the parent-mediated child mindfulness training, some effects on the mothers were apparent. Parenting stress was reduced, with statistical significance. There were increases in family quality of life, but without statistical significance. Finally, the level of mindfulness mothers reported after their own training was retained. It is difficult, however, to discern to what extent these results are indirectly caused by their role as mindfulness teacher to their own child, and to what extent they are simply the result of the continuation of their own personal practice.

Previous studies have documented the indirect effects of training carers, whether parents (e.g. Neece, 2013; Singh, Lancioni, Winton, Fisher, et al., 2006; Singh et al., 2014; Singh et al., 2007) or professional carers (e.g. Singh, Lancioni, Winton, Curtis, et al., 2006; Singh et al., 2004) on the behavioural wellbeing of those in their care. A longitudinal study also reported a reciprocal relationship between parenting stress and child problem behaviours for parents of children with developmental delays (Neece, Green, & Baker, 2012). All these results are in line with the current study.

Given the studies that have demonstrated transactional effects between care providers and care recipients when one or both parties practise mindfulness, it is possible that in this study the mindfulness training undergone by mothers, supported by their perceptions of changes in their child's challenging behaviours, may have fed back into their own psychological wellbeing. Hwang and Kearney (2014) suggested such a possibility, but to our knowledge there is no intervention study reporting such effects.

The current findings, together with those of previous studies (i.e. Bögels et al., 2013; Neece, 2013; Singh, Lancioni, Winton, Fisher, et al., 2006; Singh et al., 2014; Singh et al., 2007), suggest that the reciprocal nature of the relationships between care providers and care recipients is not restricted to difficulties, but also to the effects of mindfulness. In other words, just as the challenging behaviours of children with DD can be addressed through training their parents in mindfulness, so too it might be possible to address the psychological difficulties of parents through training their children with DD in mindfulness, to the degree they could manage their own challenging behaviours. Although the nature of this reciprocity is still in the process of being uncovered (Harnett & Dawe, 2012), there are two major areas of interest, those of improving child–parent interactions and reducing parenting stress. We believe it may be possible to empower families as a unit by training both mothers and their children with DD in mindfulness.

6.3 Critical Issues of Mindfulness Intervention for Individuals Living with DD

6.3.1 Theoretical Issues of Mindfulness Intervention for People Living with DD

In this study we decided to return to the origins of mindfulness in the teaching of the Buddha. As we discussed in Chap. 2, no existing mindfulness practice package fitted the unique aims of this study, which were to train mothers to be mindfulness teachers of their own children with ASD and challenging behaviour and then train the children themselves in partnership with their mothers. This is particularly the case since the diversity of characteristics typical of individuals with ASD means that no specific technique could be confidently assumed to apply to all these children.

The problem became one of finding a way to present mindfulness and its practice to a group of mothers that would be relevant to their daily lives and empower them to teach mindfulness to their own children. The solution we decided to implement was to train them in the fundamental principles of mindfulness practice as provided by the originator of the practice, the Buddha himself. Here we were treating the Buddha as an empirical psychologist who had something useful to say about the human condition. By returning to the framework he provided, we were able to present mothers with a training programme that was based on first principles and possessed its own theoretical and practical coherence. From these principles we were able to help them develop a sophisticated understanding of their physical and mental experience that was directly relevant to how they lived their everyday lives, including their family relationships.

The key theoretical point here was that we treated mindfulness as a unitary rather than a collective term. Following the tradition, mindfulness was defined as remembering the object of awareness. This simplicity gave us the opportunity to distinguish mindfulness from its supporting qualities, and to see how those qualities could combine and rearrange themselves to form different styles of mindfulness practice that could adapt to the individuality of each participant, whether mother or child. Rather than mastering a specific technique, mothers were trained in the craft of tracking their experience over time and communicating this experience to themselves and others.

In this way the current study has attempted to adapt the rich phenomenological tradition that begins with the Buddha to the demands of contemporary social science without compromising either science or the dharma that the Buddha taught. We have done so without taking an eclectic approach that draws from a variety of traditions and attempts to bring them into a single practice package, but by cleaving to the internal consistency that characterises the Buddha's dharma, before its evolution into a variety of different philosophical and practice traditions. This approach promises to maintain a theoretical coherence that might otherwise be compromised.

6.3.2 *Practical Issues of Mindfulness Intervention for People Living with DD*

This section discusses some practical issues concerning the project of training mothers of children with ASD and challenging behaviours and the children themselves in mindfulness practice. These are as follows: (1) the quality of the mindfulness teachers and intervention fidelity; (2) the degree of engagement in mindfulness practice, including the commitment to ongoing practice over time; and (3) the continuing levels of support for the practitioners, to maintain engagement and motivation. These issues appear to be critical in determining the success of a mindfulness intervention, for reasons outlined below.

6.3.2.1 Quality of Mindfulness Teachers and Intervention Fidelity

Teacher quality is a major concern in determining the level of engagement in mindfulness practice for children with ASD. Mindfulness teachers of individuals with DD need to understand both mindfulness and these individuals with DD in order to provide mindfulness training that accommodates the variety of educational requirements that characterise them (Hwang & Kearney, 2013). Regarding mindfulness, although intellectual knowledge is necessary to understand mindfulness and its applications, it is not enough for either teachers or students of mindfulness (Grossman, 2010). Substantial and prolonged practice of mindfulness is required for those who would teach mindfulness to others (Kabat-Zinn, 2003; Segal, Williams, & Teasdale, 2002). This requirement places special demands on the mother teachers of this intervention, as demonstrated in the practice patterns that emerged from the experience of the six mother–child dyads. Mother teachers must themselves embody mindfulness practice if they are to effectively convey it to their children.

Mindfulness teachers of individuals with DD also require an understanding of individuals with DD if they are to accommodate the wide diversity of learning requirements that often characterises this population. It is not uncommon for intervention content and learning process to require adjustment to meet the learning requirements of people with DD (Kaiser & McIntyre, 2010). Previous intervention studies (e.g. Brown & Hooper, 2009; Miodrag, Lense, & Dykens, 2013) that adopted the existing MBIs were also keenly aware of the necessity to adjust their programmes to the particular characteristics of individuals with DD. One difficulty is that such adjustments, although inevitable, may compromise intervention fidelity. This reinforces the need for mindfulness teachers in the DD community to possess high levels of knowledge of both mindfulness and disabilities.

An additional requirement for the effectiveness of mindfulness teachers in the field of disability is teacher–learner compatibility. In this study, the quality of the relationship between children with DD and their teachers played a critical role in determining the level of commitment of these children to their mindfulness practice. In the Vicky–Sam dyad, for example, Sam resisted social interactions with the researchers, and they therefore played a relatively minor role in his training. His mother was able to fill this gap, however, as Sam responded well to her as a teacher. A contrasting situation was found in the Shane–David dyad, where David, a teenage boy, resisted being instructed by his mother and preferred the sessions with the researchers, where he was fully engaged with them. While he continued his commitment after the visits by the researchers ceased, his practice finally fell away when his mother fell ill and could no longer practise with him.

6.3.2.2 Engagement in Mindfulness Intervention and Commitment to Mindfulness Practice

The second practical issue concerns engagement in the intervention and commitment to the ongoing regular mindfulness practice on the part of individuals with

DD. Disengagement and non-completion of intervention pose a major threat to the success of an intervention (Jochems et al., 2012). For mindfulness practice to have long-lasting effects, it is crucial that individuals with DD are committed to a long-term practice (Hwang & Kearney, 2013). As children with ASD normally have difficulties in engaging with learning (Keen, 2010), this kind of commitment cannot be readily expected.

Despite the importance of engagement for intervention outcomes regarding individuals with DD (Kaiser & McIntyre, 2010), we found that only a limited number of studies discussed this matter. Bögels et al. (2008), for example, reported difficulties in engaging the adolescents with externalising disorders in mindfulness training because of their problems in concentrating and their overt non-compliance. Brown and Hooper (2009) noted similar difficulties in engaging a female adolescent with DD in their mindfulness program, and Idusohan-Moizer et al. (2013) had two adults with ID drop out of the intervention because they disliked the meditation practice.

The importance of the mothers remaining engaged with their mindfulness practice was demonstrated in the patterns of the six mother–child dyads, where a necessary but not sufficient condition for children to remain engaged in their mindfulness practice was the continuing engagement of their mother teachers. This shows the importance of the role of the mother teacher in this intervention, as the engagement of children in mindfulness practice cannot be expected if their mother teacher lacks commitment. Kasari, Gulsrud, Wong, Kwon and Locke (2010) also stressed the importance of the involvement of care providers in teaching for success in care provider-implemented joint engagement interventions for children with ASD.

6.3.2.3 The Ongoing Support for Practitioners' Engagement and Motivation

The mothers also found it challenging to maintain a regular engagement with mindfulness practice, at first during the self-practice period and then for the 12-month home-based intervention period. This problem revolves around a commitment loop that affects all practitioners of mindfulness meditation. Given that the beneficial effects of mindfulness practice emerge only in the long term, a practitioner has to engage in it for a sustained period before seeing these benefits. However, in the absence of apparent benefits, it is difficult to be motivated to sustain a practice in the face of the normal demands of everyday life.

One way to deal with this difficulty lies in making mindfulness practice a social activity, creating a group of like-minded people who are engaged in the same project. During stage 1 of the intervention, when mothers were meeting together once a week, the enthusiasm with which they related to each other provided a powerful motivation to persevere with their individual practice. When subsequently left alone, however, commitment became more difficult. We helped sustain it with online and face-to-face meetings, to extend the felt sense of community that characterised the eight-week training period. It is clear that future mindfulness interventions would be aided by the development of a community of mindfulness practitioners, to provide both practice and social support for families engaged in mindfulness practice.

6.3.3 Methodological Issues of Mindfulness Intervention for People Living with DD

The methodological issues concern the design of this mindfulness intervention, where we adopted a parent-implemented mindfulness strategy for children with ASD and challenging behaviours. Inviting mothers to play a central role in training their children in mindfulness brought out a number of advantages. Despite the frequently expressed concern that taking up the extra role of teaching one's own child could exacerbate a parent's existing stress (Oono, Honey, & McConachie, 2013), mothers did not find teaching their child with ASD to be stressful. Rather, they showed that parent-implemented training could utilise some invaluable assets that parents possess, such as their understanding of their child's development and learning requirements, along with a high level of commitment to and availability for teaching (Vernon, Koegel, Dauterman, & Stolen, 2012, p. 2703). In this study, the anticipation that they would be delivering mindfulness training to their child motivated mothers in their own practice. More importantly, training mothers to become teachers of their own children empowered them, as it helped build their capacity to teach their children (Matson, Mahan, & Matson, 2009). Mothers said that training their children with ASD in mindfulness was like extending their existing parenting and teaching skill set.

The parent-implemented intervention design, however, did present challenges. Kaiser and Hancock (2003) had previously warned that not all parents are ready and willing to learn new strategies to teach their children, and this would influence intervention effects. Indeed, in this current study not all mothers completed their parent-implemented child mindfulness training, because of the challenge of a lack of time and energy (Kaiser & Hancock, 2003). One key to maintaining parent-implemented mindfulness training was found in the mothers' understanding of the benefits of their own mindfulness practice. This allowed them to persevere in their implementation of the intervention for their child despite the challenges regarding time and energy.

We also found that not every child was ready and willing to learn from his or her parent. The age of child practitioners ranged between 8 years and 15 years, and parent-implemented training seemed to be better received by the younger rather than the older children. We found the two youngest children demonstrated the most noticeable reductions in their challenging behaviours. As children grow, the nature of the parent–child relationship changes. When children enter the teenage period, for example, they become more independent in their learning and living. Learning new strategies to address one's challenging behaviours from one's own mother may not be the best learning arrangement. The results of a review of 456 intervention studies for children, youth and young adults with ASD reflected this age factor, indicating parent-implemented interventions to their child with ASD were effective especially for toddlers (0–2 years) to primary school-aged learners (6–11 years) (Wong et al., 2013).

6.4 Limitations of the Study

The current study has several limitations. The first is the small number of participants. There was no control group, and although recruitment was widely advertised, a possibility of sampling bias cannot be ruled out. These factors significantly limit not only the capacity to demonstrate the effects of the intervention objectively but also the generalisation of the findings (Charman & Howlin, 2003). Non-completion of the intervention is another limitation, as of the six mother–child dyads in the study one did not complete the parent-mediated child mindfulness training. The reliance on mothers as teachers can also be seen as a limitation, as one child discontinued mindfulness practice in part because of his problematic relationship with his mother teacher.

The measurement of the effects of mindfulness training was also problematic. The effects of mindfulness training were measured through self-reported questionnaires, and mothers completed these for themselves and their children. It is possible, therefore, that the results may reflect changes in the perceptions of mothers, rather than in the actual behaviour of themselves and their children. To address this problem, we initially asked mothers to record the frequencies of their children's behaviours, with family members responsible for reliability checking. However, this practice was discontinued during the intervention period, as mothers found it too demanding, for themselves and their families.

Another limitation lies in the difficulty of distinguishing discrete causal trajectories, establishing which specific cause gives rise to a given result. For example, one of the direct effects of parent mindfulness training was increased family quality of life, but this might be explained by the opportunity that mothers had to get away from their family and spend time together to nurture themselves. Also, the indirect effects of the parent-implemented mindfulness training on the mothers may be the result of factors other than the mindfulness training itself, such as the quality of the family time generated by mothers teaching their children. Our intervention has no way of disentangling these distinct lines of cause and effect.

Last but not least is the difficulty in measuring mindfulness. While the mothers were trained on the basis of a conception of mindfulness taken directly from the early tradition, we relied on a self-report questionnaire created on the basis of the understanding of mindfulness in contemporary psychology (Grossman, 2011). This mismatch needs to be addressed in future studies. For all these reasons, the results of this study can only be considered indicative, and they need to be interpreted with great caution.

6.5 Implications for Future Research

Despite these limitations, this study builds on and extends from the existing mindfulness research literature in ASD. It adds to our understanding of the nature of the reciprocal relationships between parent mindfulness practice and child challenging behaviours on the one hand, and child mindfulness practice and parenting stress on the other. This study has also examined the feasibility of training mothers to become mindfulness teachers of their own children with ASD, and it explored the application of recent education theories and practices (e.g. differentiation, self-determination, universal design for learning, video modelling) to the development and implementation of parent-implemented child mindfulness training.

The individuality of people with ASD gives rise to a wide variety of responses to intervention content and process. This implies that a high level of knowledge regarding mindfulness and disability is necessary to equip people to become mindfulness teachers of people with ASD. Future studies may look at applying a multidisciplinary approach, where professionals with different skills and expertise work together for the common goal of enhancing the psychological and/or behavioural wellbeing of people living with ASD. The practice of mindfulness occurs within one's own body and mind, so it cannot be externally imposed. In addition, for mindfulness practice to yield long-lasting effects for individuals with DD, long-term practice is required on their part (Hwang & Kearney, 2013). However, as children with ASD are typically not fully engaged in learning (Keen, 2010), future studies could investigate the optimal conditions that would serve to enhance the motivation and engagement of learners and teachers in mindfulness training.

In addition, we learned from our systematic review of mindfulness intervention studies that more research attention is being given to the psychological wellbeing of individuals with ASD than was the case formerly, when the focus was on the behavioural wellbeing of individuals with ID. We found that the existing mindfulness-based intervention programmes that were initially developed for individuals without DD were being adjusted to meet the learning requirements and distinctive characteristics of individuals with DD. Future studies could also look at the adjustments to intervention content and process required for this transition.

Another area for future study involves how mindfulness practice influences the reciprocal relationships between parents and children (Bögels et al., 2013). One way forward would be through reliance on qualitative approaches to researching the effects of mindfulness training (Bluth, Roberson, Billen, & Sams, 2013; Grossman, 2011). The reflections of mindfulness practitioners on their inner experience may reveal more of how family relationships are affected by mindfulness training, and how and why individuals respond differently to the same mindfulness training.

As ASD is a life-long condition, cost-effectiveness is particularly important, along with influences on quality of life (Charman & Howlin, 2003). It follows that training parents has a particular appeal (Matson et al., 2009). Another issue concerns the role of fathers. Most studies that examine the effects of parent mindfulness training include mothers but not fathers. As fathers have different perceptions of their children (Bluth et al., 2013), form different relationships with them and have different experiences of parenting stress (Neece et al., 2012), future studies that train children with ASD in mindfulness could look at making more effort to encourage fathers to participate.

In the current study mothers acknowledged the importance of the ongoing regular mindfulness practice for themselves and their children, yet they had difficulty in engaging in long-term practice. For parents of children with ASD and challenging behaviours, future studies could look at the roles of parent support groups for motivating an ongoing commitment to practice.

Continuing with the need for social support, future studies could also investigate using parent-implemented mindfulness training as an early intervention to provide support for parents of very young children with ASD. Given the stresses parents undergo when they are caught up with worries over their children with ASD (Russell, 2011), especially during a child's diagnosis and transition periods (Neece et al., 2012; Silva and Schalock, 2012), a socially supported intervention aimed at that stage may be very useful for family wellbeing. This is especially so when younger children may be more responsive to the changes in their environment brought on by the increased mindfulness of their parents. Peer-supported mindfulness practice may also be effective in school settings, where children with ASD could practise with others and thus normalise both their practice and the experiences that arise from their practice.

6.6 Conclusion

The defining questions of this study concern what happens to individuals with DD when they practise mindfulness, and what happens to individuals with DD when their family or professional care providers practise mindfulness. We conducted a two-stage mindfulness intervention, parent mindfulness training and parent-implemented child mindfulness training, to address these questions. We thought it probable that the family as a unit could be strengthened and empowered during this intervention process.

The results of the intervention show some positive training effects on mothers and their children with ASD and challenging behaviours. These findings, together with the results of the systematic review of mindfulness interventions, suggest that people with DD can learn and practise mindfulness to help them address their own behavioural and/or psychological difficulties. Mindfulness may also be used indirectly, to help individuals with DD who may not yet be ready to learn it, by training their family or professional care providers.

Given that the direct benefits of mindfulness practice require a commitment to its practice over time, and such commitment presents difficulties to people regardless of disabilities, community support is very important for both children with ASD and their parents in mindfulness interventions. The role of community in mindfulness practice, however, goes deeper than the issues of support for individual practice. The results of this two-staged mindfulness intervention suggest that the presence of reciprocal relationships between parents and children affects access to the benefits of mindfulness practice. As discussed in Chap. 5, the mindfulness practice of the mothers had a beneficial effect on their children with ASD in terms of their behavioural and psychological wellbeing, and the parent-implemented mindfulness practice of these children may have had a beneficial effect on their mothers in terms of their psychological wellbeing.

The effects of mindfulness practice on behaviour are, by their nature, indirect. Mindfulness does not directly affect behaviour, but rather the mind that produces behaviour. Given the complexity of each human mind, the effects of mindfulness training can vary greatly from one person to another. The network of relationships that emerge between individual human minds is even more complex. We could say that mindfulness creates possibilities, both individual and social, rather than easily identified certainties. We therefore call for more studies to investigate the wide range of possible applications for mindfulness practice, with particular attention to the developmental trajectories that move from changes in the mind to changes in behaviour, both individually and socially. All we have done in this study is plant some seeds for future research in this field.

References

Bazzano, A., Wolfe, C., Zylowska, L., Wang, S., Shchuster, E., Barrett, C., & Lehrer, D. (2013). Mindfulness based stress reduction (MBSR) for parents and caregivers of individuals with developmental disabilities: A comunity-based approach. *Journal of Child Family Studies*. doi:10.1007/s10826-013-9836-9

Benn, R., Akiva, T., Arel, S., & Roeser, R. (2012). Mindfulness training effects for parents and educators of children with special needs. *Developmental Psychology, 48,* 1476–1487.

Blackledge, J. T., & Hayes, S. C. (2006). Using acceptance and commitment training in the support of parents of children diagnosed with autism. *Child & Family Behaviour Therapy, 28*(1), 1–18.

Bluth, K., Roberson, P., Billen, R., & Sams, J. (2013). A stress model for couples parenting children with autism spectrum disorders and the introduction of a Mindfulness intervention. *Journal of Family Theory & Review, 5,* 194–213.

Bögels, S., Hoogstad, B., van Dun, L., de Schutter, S., & Restifo, K. (2008). Mindfulness training for adolescents with externalising disorders and their parents. *Behavioural and Cognitive Psychotherapy, 36,* 193–209.

Bögels, S., Lehtonen, A., & Restifo, K. (2010). Mindful Parenting in mental health care *Mindfulness, 1,* 107–120.

Bögels, S., Hellemans, J., Deursen, S. v., Römer, M., & Meulen, R. v. d. (2013). Mindful parenting in mental health care: Effects on parental and child psychology, parental stress, parenting, coparenting, and marital functioning. *Mindfulness*. doi:10.1007/s12671-013-0209-7

Brown, F. J., & Hooper, S. (2009). Acceptance and commitment therapy (ACT) with a learning disabled young person experiencing anxious and obsessive thoughts. *Journal of Intellectual Disabilities, 13,* 195–201.

Charman, T., & Howlin, P. (2003). Research into early intervention for children with autism and related disorders: Methodological and design issues. *Autism, 7,* 217–225.

Coatsworth, D., Duncan, L., Greenberg, M., & Nix, R. (2010). Changing parent's mindfulness, child management skills and relationship quality with their youth: Results from a randomized pilot intervention trial. *Journal of Child Family Studies, 19,* 203–217.

Dumas, J. (2005). Mindfulness-based parent training: Strategies to lessen the grip of automaticity in families with disruptive children. *Journal of Clinical Child & Adolescent Psychology, 34,* 779–791.

Ferraioli, S., & Harris, S. (2013). Comparative effects of mindfulness and skills-based parent training programs for parents of children with autism: Feasibility and preliminary outcome data. *Mindfulness, 4,* 89–101.

Grossman, P. (2010). Mindfulness for psychologists: Paying kind attention to the perceptible. *Mindfulness, 1,* 87–97.

Grossman, P. (2011). Defining mindfulness by how poorly I think I pay attention during everyday awareness and other intractable problems for psychology's (Re)invention of mindfulness: Comment on Brown et al. (2011). *Psychological Assessment, 23*(4), 1034–1040.

Harnett, P., & Dawe, S. (2012). Review: The contribution of mindfulness-based therapies for children and families and proposed conceptual integration. *Child and Adolescent Mental Health, 17*(4), 195–208.

Hoffman, L., Marquis, J. G., Poston, D. J., Summers, J. A., & Turnbull, A. (2006). Assessing family outcomes: Psychometric evaluation of the family quality of life scale. *Journal of Marriage and Family, 68,* 1069–1083.

Hwang, Y. S., & Kearney, P. (2013). A systematic review of mindfulness intervention for individuals with developmental disabilities: Long-term practice and long lasting effects. *Research in Developmental Disabilities, 34,* 314–326.

Hwang, Y. S., & Kearney, P. (2014). Mindful and mutual care for individuals with developmental disabilities: A systematic literature review. *Journal of Child Family Studies, 23*(3), 497–509. doi:10.1007/s10826-012-9707-9

Idusohan-Moizer, H., Sawicka, A., Dendle, J., & Albany, M. (2013). Mindfulness-based cognitive therapy for adults with intellectual disabilities: An evaluation of the effectiveness of mindfulness in reducing symptoms of depression and anxiety. *Journal of Intellectual Disability Research,* 1–12. doi:10.1111/jir.12082

Jochems, E. C., Mulder, C. L., Dam, A. v., Duivenvoorden, H. J., Scheffer, S. C., Spek, W. v. d., & Feltz-Cornelis, C. M. v. d. (2012). Motivation and treatment engagement intervention trial (MotivaTe-IT): The effects of motivation feedback to clinicians on treatment engagement in patients with severe mental illness. *BMC Psychiatry, 12,* 209–216.

Kabat-Zinn, J. (2003). Mindfulness-based interventions in context: Past, present, and future. *Clinical Psychology: Science and Practice, 10,* 144–156.

Kaiser, A. P., & Hancock, T. B. (2003). Teaching parents new skills to support their young children's development. *Infants & Young Children, 16,* 9–21.

Kaiser, A. P., & McIntyre, L. L. (2010). Introduction to special section on evidence-based practices for persons with intellectual and developmental disabilities. *American Journal on Intellectual and Developmental Disabilities, 115,* 357–363.

Kasari, C., Gulsrud, A. C., Wong, C., Kwon, S., & Locke, J. (2010). Randomized controlled caregiver mediated joint engagement intervention for toddlers with autism. *Journal of Autism and Developmental Disorders, 40,* 1045–1056.

Keen, D. (2010). Engagement of children with autism in learning. *Australasian Journal of Special Education, 33*(2), 130–140.

MacDonald, E. E., & Hastings, R. P. (2008). Mindful parenting and care involvement of fathers of children with intellectual disabilities. *Journal of Child Family Studies.* doi:10.1007/s10826-008-9243-9.

Matson, M., Mahan, S., & Matson, J. (2009). Parent training: A review of methods for children with autism spectrum disorders. *Research in Autism Spectrum Disorders, 3,* 868–875.

Miodrag, N., Lense, M. D., & Dykens, E. M. (2013). A pilot study of mindfulness intervention for individuals with Williams syndrome: Physiological outcomes. *Mindfulness, 4,* 137–147.

Neece, C. (2013). Mindfulness-based stress reduction for parents of young children with developmental delays: Implications for parental mental health and child behaviour problems. *Journal of Applied Research in Intellectual Disabilities.* doi:10.1111/jar.12064

Neece, C., Green, S., & Baker, B. (2012). Parenting stress and child behavior problems: A transactional relationship across time. *American Journal on Intellectual and Developmental Disabilities, 117,* 48–66.

Oono, I. P., Honey, E. J., & McConachie, H. (2013). Parent-mediated early intervention for young children with autism spectrum disorders (ASD). *Evidence-Based Child Health, 8*(6), 2380–2479.

Russell, J. (2011). Mindfulness: A tool for parents and children with Asperger's Syndrome. *Mindfulness, 2,* 212–215.

Segal, Z. V., Williams, J. M. G., & Teasdale, J. D. (2002). *Mindfulness-based cognitive therapy for depression: A new approach to preventing relapse*. New York: Guilford.

Silva, L., & Schalock, M. (2012). Autism parenting stress index: Initial psychometric evidence. *Journal of Autism and Developmental Disorders, 42,* 566–574.

Singh, N. N., Lancioni, G. E., Winton, A. S. W., Wahler, R. G., Singh, J., & Sage, M. (2004). Mindful caregiving increases happiness among individuals with profound multiple disabilities. *Research in Developmental Disabilities, 25,* 207–218.

Singh, N. N., Lancioni, G. E., Winton, A. S. W., Curtis, W. J., Wahler, R. G., Sabaawi, M., Singh, J., McAleavey, K., et al. (2006a). Mindful staff increase learning and reduce aggression in adults with developmental disabilities. *Research in Developmental Disabilities, 27,* 545–558.

Singh, N. N., Lancioni, G. E., Winton, A. S. W., Fisher, B. C., Wahler, R. G., McAleavey, K., Singh, J., SaBaawi, M., et al. (2006b). Mindful parenting decreases aggression, noncompliance, and self-injury in children with autism. *Journal of Emotional and Behavioural Disorders, 14*(3), 169–177.

Singh, N. N., Lancioni, G. E., Winton, A. S. W., Singh, J., Curtis, W. J., Wahler, R. G., & McAleavey, K. M. (2007). Mindful parenting decreases aggression and increases social behaviour in children with developmental disabilities. *Behaviour Modification, 31,* 749–771.

Singh, N. N., Lancioni, G. E., Winton, A. S. W., Singh, A. N. A., Adkins, A. D. A., & Singh, J. (2009). Mindful staff can reduce the use of physical restraints when providing care to individuals with intellectual disabilities. *Journal of Applied Research in Intellectual Disabilities, 22,* 194–202.

Singh, N. N., Lancioni, G. E., Manikam, R., Winton, A. S. W., Singh, A. N. A., Singh, J., & Singh, A. D. A. (2011a). A mindfulness-based strategy for self-management of aggressive behaviour in adolescents with autism. *Research in Autism Spectrum Disorders, 5,* 1153–1158.

Singh, N. N., Lancioni, G. E., Singh, A. D. A., Winton, A. S. W., Singh, A. N. A., & Singh, J. (2011b). Adolescents with asperger syndrome can use a mindfulness-based strategy to control their aggressive behaviour. *Research in Autism Spectrum Disorders, 5,* 1103–1109.

Singh, N. N., Lancioni, G. E., Winton, A. S. W., Karazsia, B. T., Myers, R. E., Latham, L. I., & Singh, J. (2014). Mindfulness-based positive behavior support (MBPBS) for mothers of adolescents with autism spectrum disorder: Effects on adolescents' behavior and parental stress. *Mindfulness*. doi:10.1007/s12671-014-0321-3.

Spek, A., van Ham, N., & Nyklicek, I. (2013). Mindfulness-based therapy in adults with an autism spectrum disorder: A randomized controlled trial. *Research in Developmental Disabilities, 34*(1), 246–253.

Vernon, T. W., Koegel, R. L., Dauterman, H., & Stolen, K. (2012). An early social engagement intervention for young children with autism and their parents. *Journal of Autism and Developmental Disorders, 42,* 2702–2717.

Wong, C., Odom, S. L., Hume, K., Cox, A. W., Fettig, A., Kucharczyk, S., Schultz, T. R., et al. (2013). *Evidence-based practices for children, youth, and young adults with Autism Spectrum Disorder*. Chapel Hill The University of North Carolina, Frank Porter Graham Child Development Institute, Autism Evidence-Based Practice Review Group.

Appendices

Appendix 1: Five Basic Mindfulness Exercises

Figure 8

Stand or sit with your hands hanging, and relax.
Leading from your wrist, slowly lift one hand up to your shoulder.
Leading from your wrist, wave your hand in a figure 8.
Slowly make the 8 bigger …, bigger …, and bigger.
Then slowly make the 8 smaller …, smaller …, and smaller …
When the 8 becomes very small, bring your hand down to your tummy.
Leading from your wrist, slowly lift the other hand up to your shoulder.
Leading from your wrist, wave your hand in a figure 8.
Slowly make the 8 bigger …, bigger …, and bigger.
Then slowly make the 8 smaller …, smaller …, and smaller …
When the 8 becomes very small, bring your hand down to your other hand.
Feel any movement on your tummy as you breathe, and relax (20 s).
Continue to feel the movement, and relax (20 s).
Smile, and thank yourself.

Waving

Stand or sit with your hands hanging, and relax.
Leading from your wrists, slowly wave your hands up to shoulder height.
Slowly wave your hands down.
Slowly wave your hands up.
Wave down; wave up.
Slowly and gently …
The waves become smaller … and smaller … and smaller …

Y.-S. Hwang, P. Kearney, *A Mindfulness Intervention for Children with Autism Spectrum Disorder*, Mindfulness in Behavioral Health,
DOI 10.1007/978-3-319-18962-8

Bring your hands to rest on your tummy.
Feel any movement on your tummy as you breathe, and relax.
Continue to feel the movement, and relax.
Smile, and thank yourself.

Cat Walking

Stand with your feet as wide as your shoulders. Look down, and see if you can make a number 11 with your feet.

Bend your knees slightly, and relax.

Swing your weight onto one foot. Slowly step out with your other foot, and touch the floor with the front of the foot, behind your toes. Drop your foot down, feeling the floor. Then slide forward onto that foot, quietly, like a cat!

Your foot behind you becomes lighter. Lift it up, step out, and touch the floor with the front of your foot. Drop your foot down, feeling the floor. Then slide forward onto that foot, quietly, like a cat!

Lift your back foot, step out, touch the floor, and slide forward.
Lift your back foot, step out, touch the floor, and slide forward.
Continue to walk around the room like a cat Lift, touch, slide.
Come back into standing, with your feet as wide as your shoulders.
Feel the ground against your feet.
Continue to feel the ground, and relax.
Smile, and thank yourself.

Lion Lying

Lie down on your back with your hands resting on your tummy, and relax.
Relax your whole body.
Feel the ground on the back of your legs.
Feel how your body moves, as you breathe in; as you breathe out.
Relax.
Feel the ground against your hips.
Feel how your body moves, as you breathe in; as you breathe out.
Relax.
Feel the ground against your back.
Feel how your body moves, as you breathe in; as you breathe out.
Relax.
Feel the ground against your arms.
Feel how your body moves, as you breathe in; as you breathe out.
Relax.
Feel the ground against your head.

Feel how your body moves, as you breathe in; as you breathe out.
Relax.
Feel the ground against your whole body.
Feel how your body moves, as you breathe in; as you breathe out.
Relax.
Relax your face.
Smile, and thank yourself.

Sounds

Sit comfortably.
Breath in. Breath out. Relax.
Listen. What can you hear? *(Sounding bell.)*
Let the sound go straight through. Relax.
(Sounding bell.) Can you tell when the sound stops?
Listen again. When does the sound stop? *(Sounding bell.)*
Let the sound go straight through. Relax.
Listen to the sounds around you. What can you hear now?
Let the sounds go straight through. Relax.
Smile, and thank yourself.

Appendix 2: Three Additional Mindfulness Activities

Mindfulness of Mind

Clouds

Imagine your mind is like the sky, open, wide, and clear.

Are you thinking? Imagine your thoughts as clouds, moving through the sky.

The thought clouds may be bright, or they may be dark. They may be light, or they may be heavy.

Let the thoughts move through the sky. Do not get in their way. Do not try to hold on to them, or to stop them. Just let them come, and let them go.

Behind the clouds, the sky is still open, wide, and clear.

Ocean

Imagine your mind is like the ocean, wide and open.

Are you thinking? Imagine your thoughts as waves on the ocean, always moving, always restless.

The thought waves may be gentle, or they may be rough. They may be strong, or they may be weak.

Let the waves come and go. Do not get in their way. Do not dive into them. Just let them come and let them go.

When a wave is gone, it leaves nothing behind. Just the wide, open ocean.

Pleasant and Painful Feelings

Look at your mind, and the thoughts flowing through them.

Are you thinking? What do thoughts feel like?

Are some thoughts pleasant? Do you enjoy them?

Are some thoughts painful? Do you want them to go away?

When a thought is pleasant, just name it "pleasant," and let it go, like a cloud passing through the sky.

When a thought is painful, just name it "painful," and let it go, like a cloud passing through the sky.

Can you notice the spaces between the thoughts? Is the mind peaceful and still, there?

Family Loving-Kindness Exercise

(This exercise was performed with a small singing bowl and a wooden mallet.)

Sit in a circle.

Make yourself comfortable.

This is a new mind gym activity developed to make an awesome mind. First, we will be mindful of kindness; and then we will do a kindness exercise together.

There are "must do" things in this exercise.

Whoever is holding this mallet is the one who speaks. We will each take a turn to hold this mallet. When one of us speaks, we just listen to that person, without interrupting him or her and with our full attention.

While we listen, we nod our head at that person to show we are listening.

We first talk about a time when we felt hurt by others.

Then we talk about a time when we hurt others, and talk about our regret about that time.

The next person will get the mallet and do the same thing.

When everyone is done, we draw a symbol of our own hurt and a symbol of the hurt of other people.

We put the drawings into the bowl.

We will send kindness to heal our own hurt and the hurt of others.

Afterwards we will throw away the drawings, and with them we will throw away all our own hurt and the hurt of others.

Let us begin our mindfulness of kindness.

Mindfulness of kindness
May I be happy.
May I be free from pain.
May I be in peace.
May all of us be happy.
May all of us be free from pain.
May all of us be in peace.
May our family, friends, and relatives be happy.
May they be free from pain.
May they be in peace.
May everyone be happy.
May everyone be free from pain.
May everyone be in peace.

(The group exercise follows, after which the papers that contain drawings of our hurt and the hurt of others is taken by all and either thrown away or burned.)

Meditation on Anger/Worry

Sit or lie down.

Feel the floor underneath you, or your cushion or your bench. Feel the hardness of it.

Now put your hands on your tummy.
Feel your hands.
Is your tummy moving as you breathe?
If it is moving, feel the movements.
Think of a time when you were angry, or worried.
Remember where you were.
Remember who you were with.
Remember what happened.
You may feel angry, or worried. That is okay.

It is okay to be angry or worried, as long as you know that you are angry or worried.

Now do not think about that any more.
Instead, feel your hands on your tummy.
Is your tummy moving as you breathe?
If it is moving, feel the movements.
Do not worry about anything.
Just feel your hands and tummy.
And now smile. Pat your shoulder and thank yourself.

Index

Y.-S. Hwang, P. Kearney, *A Mindfulness Intervention for Children with Autism Spectrum Disorder*, Mindfulness in Behavioral Health,
DOI 10.1007/978-3-319-18962-8

MIX
Papier aus verantwortungsvollen Quellen
Paper from responsible sources
FSC® C105338

Printed by Books on Demand, Germany